I0199648

JOURNEY OF SOUL-LED ENDEAVOURS

Through The Eyes of An Infantry Officer

Autobiography Of Robert Honey

EDITED TRANSCRIPT OF ORIGINAL MANUSCRIPT

BY CHANTELLE HONEY

First Edition

978-0-6456908-0-4

Disclaimer: This is an autobiography. The events are portrayed to the best of Robert Honey's memory. While all the stories in this book are true, some names and identifying details have been changed to protect the privacy of the people involved.

The conversations in the book all come from the author's recollections, though they are not written to represent word-for-word transcripts. Rather, the author has retold them in a way that evokes the feeling and meaning around what was said and, in all instances, the essence of the dialogue is accurate.

This book is dedicated to:

Robert Honey – Thank you for leaving behind this extravagant piece of history, and always striving to follow his soul.

In remembrance of Georgie Honey, who was only on this earth for a short time but will now be remembered with every opening of this book.

Dedications also go out to Peter Honey, who at times can be as stubborn as a turtle on a lap, but has given insight, honesty and support when needed. Thank you for your dedication, guidance, and intelligence. *Supplied and edited by Peter J Honey.*

Table of Contents

PREFACE:

Giving you a glimpse into World War 1 and the endeavours that followed, this autobiography and collection of memoirs are written through the eyes of an infantry soldier as he navigates war, abandonment, betrayal, loss, and love.

Beginning in England, Robert shares his inspirational story demonstrating what life was like during The Great War.

From early childhood memories to Navy adventures, joining the Australian Imperial Forces, everyman to France, the Armistice to Soldier settlements and rapid agricultural development in Australia, this book is an eclectic historical time warp that is sure to draw tears, raise gratitude and provide faith.

INTRODUCTION: FAMILY HISTORY IN ENGLAND

Robert Honey, born 6/3/1900 in London, England. These memoirs commenced on the 6/2/1981.

I was born in a house in Wood Street, London. It is a street turning off from the Lambeth walk, beside the railway arches. The railway arches were used as stables by the Mineral Water Manufacturers 'Plowman + Barrett', of which, at that time, my father was a horse keeper. He later became a carman traveller for the same firm; this means that he drove a heavy two horse wagon loaded with various soft drinks and syphons of soda water, lithia and other mineral waters. He delivered these to various customers around the Greater London area, trying to entice new customers at the same time.

His father- my grandfather (Tom Honey), was a boot maker and a repairer (an exceptionally good one). All work was done by hand and his workshop was in the front room of the house that he had owned on Wickham Street. Grandmother was his assistant and old Tom Honey was known and respected throughout the trade.

My mother was the youngest daughter of Henry Marsh, who was responsible for the design and development of the coin in the slot gas meter. I never knew my maternal grandmother and I fancy that mum had been ostracized for marrying a common soldier - which dad was at the time.

The gas meter firm was taken over by the Cowans and mothers' eldest brother; Uncle Harry-who was the managing director.

CHAPTER ONE: EARLIEST MEMORIES

My earliest memory is of playing horses in Wickham Street, London, with my brother Georgie. He pretended to be the horse and me the driver. We had wooden knitted reins, made by mum through a cotton wheel. The passage of the house was a step below street level and dad had made a gate to fit in the doorway to stop us getting into the street. We were both dressed in frocks and had our hair rolled into 1 big curl on top of our heads: as was the fashion then. Apparently, we had managed to get the gate free, and we were using it as a ramp down into the passage.

I remember driving Georgie down the ramp and I think he fell. My memory of the incident stops there, and I never saw Georgie again, that I remember.

My next memory is of sitting on the floor - still in frocks, in the infants' section of the Vauxhall Street School, which had a back entrance to Wickham Street. The teacher was Mrs. Dunston and we played on the floor around her skirts.

Then came the big day when the frocks were discarded. I was britched in a velvet suit and stood on the table with Grandfather, Grandmother and Aunt Alice Honey - dad's youngest sister. Also standing alongside Mum and Dad.

I was 3 years old when mum took me around to Aunt Eliza on Sunday. Aunt Eliza had married Woodhall and Polly Woodhall, a great friend of my mother's, was my godmother. So, I figure that I must have been christened in St Mary church on Black Princes Road - as it is now. In my day it was just Princes Road.

Then I became aware of brother Alf who is 6 years older. I had known of him before, but I don't remember seeing much of him or my even older brother Will.

I only have this awareness of Alf because he threw an inkwell at his teacher, Mr. Leach, and that had caused an uproar. Then I was in the first class continuing to the second class and I also happened to do something that had annoyed Mrs. Leach. I badly wanted to go to the toilet, and I was too shy to say so, I was holding myself as not to wet my pants, but she took me out and thrashed me unmercifully and more so because I had naturally wet my pants. I was of course sent home and mum when she saw my back and buttocks was horrified. She went on to call dad-who at that time was keeping the horses in a stable at the top end of Wickham Street - the arches having been abandoned on account of the trains. He immediately marched me up to the school to the head mistress - a Mrs. Foster - he stripped me in front of her and showed her the welts left by the canes. Mrs. Leach was called in and as dad said, "if she would have been a man, he would have knocked her down". I don't know what had happened after that, but I was shifted into 3rd class and when Christmas came - into 4th class. I would then have been 7 or 8. I then skipped one class and went straight into 6th class. I was there for 2 years as I was too young to go higher.

At 11 years old I went straight into year 7. There I stayed until I was 13. In my 13th year, I was placed with 2 other boys: Billy and Tommy, at one end of the year 7th classroom. We were denoted as ex 7th as there were no higher classes to which we could be promoted, as higher education could only be obtained by means of a scholarship and you could only sit for those in your 13th year.

Our teacher was Mr. Clarke, an oxford graduate who also had a diploma in science. He was a very dedicated and fine man, and we were very fond of him.

We three boys were great chums and were used as monitors, or as they say, prefects. If a teacher was absent, we were often sent along to look after the class.

It was about 1913 when they pulled down the old church style school and rebuilt it in a hideous design, which we called 'The Cruef'. As it was a huge base with 4 tipped roof towers on each corner.

This was an exciting time for us as the work was done a bit at a time, and since the area had originally been a swamp and part of the Old Lambeth marshes. All sorts of things came to light as the area was dug out, piles growing. An old Roman Galley was dug out underneath the eastern part of the old playground.

At this time, I was attending carpentry classes. First, 1 day a week up to 13 years old. Then 2 days a week and at nights I was off to cabinet making classes. Also, we three boys, when we turned 13, were entered for the L.C.C scholarships, of which three were given each year to the boys with the highest exam marks but only one boy from a school could win. Mr. Clarke entered our names in the belief that one of us would win one of the scholarships. These were tenable at Winchester college for three years and 75 euro a year was provided by the London County Council, who controlled all schools. To that end, we would meet Mr. Clarke at the Beaufort Institute on the corner of Vauxhall Street and Princes Road each Saturday morning, and he would coach us thoroughly in all the subjects which would be likely to be covered by the exam.

When the day came, I think it was sometime in August 1913. We traveled to the Battersea Polytechnic Institute. This is where the exam was held, each boy was ushered into a glass cubicle and was given the papers, one at a time. A certain time was allocated for each paper and in my case, I always finished them well before the time, as I had never had any trouble learning. I was also an avid reader.

At last, it was finished, and we went back to our homes and respective schools. Needless to say, we were on tenterhooks waiting for the results which did not come out until over a month later. When they did, Mr. Clarke was absolutely delighted, I had topped the list with Tommy Curtis and Billy Walker in equal second phase and only a mark behind, no other school came anywhere near. The L.C.C was faced with a dilemma; the rules stated that the scholarships had to be awarded to the three schools whose scholars had the highest marks. Vauxhill street school had "scooped the pool". The council then decided that the only fair thing to do was to issue two special scholarships to Curtis and Walker.

This is where the catch came, the scholarships commenced at 18 years of age and for 14 years old to 18 years old, the winners had to attend daily at the Battersea Polytechnic. Here, they would receive suitable education, preparatory to entering Winchester. As mum and dad simply could not afford to feed and clothe me, as well as pay for my fees to and from Battersea 5 days a week for 4 years. We had to inform Mr. Black that we could not accept the scholarship. He was naturally very disappointed and as I was unable to understand mum and dad's attitude at the time, - or wouldn't understand, I became very disgruntled.

It was decided by the L.C.C that no further good could come out of my stay at school, so I was released in the winter holidays.

A friend of Will's got me a job at Pinches and Son, medalists and die sinkers. I was the office boy, Charlie; Will's friend, was the clerk. In my first week, I ran messages and was given the task to go over to the strand to collect gold and silver for the manufacture of medals. I was always amazed at the tremendous number of medals that they got out of little nuggets of gold. I was very naïve and did not know that there was only enough gold to give the color, the rest was base metal of some kind.

Around March 1914, Mr. Ernest Pinches, a nephew of the owner started working with us. My boss and I didn't like him at all and when he asked, or rather, told me to take the mail up to Vauxhill P.O as the Lambeth P.O was shut by the time the mail was ready – I was not pleased as it meant walking miles out of my way. Pinches was on the embarkment near Lambeth bridge and Vauxhill P.O up near Vauxhill bridge. This meant that I would have to walk all the way back again and then home, almost to Kennington Cross. We had moved from Wickham Street to a bigger house in Doris Street and then relocated to Princes Road as grandfather had died and grandmother had a stroke and went to live with Aunt Eliza.

I asked Mr. Ernest if I would be paid overtime, he was outraged, "overtime" he said "whoever heard of such a thing, you will do as you are told or find another job and no reference either" he snorted and walked away. I said nothing and went my way home. I dropped all of the mail into the P.O box at Lambeth. It was all stamped, so he knew nothing about it but the following week. I think on my 14th birthday week, I was cleaning out some drawers when I found a 4-inch cornered file. I asked Charlie what I would do with it, and he said to throw it away as it was worn out. I asked if I could have it, he said it was no use but if I wanted to, I could have it. I slipped it into my overcoat pocket and apparently it had worked its way through the lining and down to the front corner of the coat, between the lining and the cloth. I promptly forgot all about it; what little things change our lives!

Late one day later, I was walking home along Princes Road. It was blowing a gale and I had to cross Vauxhill Street up, which the wind was funneling. As I did so, the wind caught the front of the coat, pulled it up and out and slammed it back against my legs. I felt a sudden sharp pain and couldn't bend my right leg. I managed to pull myself along by grasping the garden railings bordering the street and eventually arriving at home.

When mum opened the door, I almost fell in. she asked what was wrong, I told her "Nothing much" and went straight up to bed. She followed me and again asked what was wrong. I said, "I don't know, something struck my leg", I had completely forgotten about the file. When dad came up, he walked upstairs, and I told him what had happened. He looked at the inside of my right knee but could only see a little blue mark

The next morning, mum borrowed a wheelchair from somewhere and wheeled me up to St Thomas hospital on the embarkment. They x-rayed the knee and found that the file had entered under the bone above the tendon and broken into two pieces. One piece broken into 1 ½ and the other piece into 1/2. They decided that they would have to operate, they did not do this for one month as the pieces were in a bad position and they had to wait for them to move. In the meantime, I was put in a metal trough splint which was angled to suit my leg, thus, on the Sunday after admission to the hospital, Charlie came to see me. He brought some fruit and informed me that Mr. Ernest had a message for me, stating that as I was unable to come to work, I was sacked. These were the good old days!

I had spent three months in the hospital, and I was only sent home on crutches as they were expecting war and they had started to build huts between the wards on the lawns. Then came the war and Alf was called up, he was in the territorials and Will joined R.H.A (Royal Horse Artillery) as a corporal saddler, he was an artificial arm and leg maker by trade. Attending the hospital daily to massage and manipulate the leg returning to normal. I obtained a position on the staff of Eyre & Spottiswoode as a copy reader, preparatory to becoming an apprentice printer. I didn't care much for this job as the reader, and we were enclosed in a small glass cubicle, and he was a boozer. His breath stank like beer, and he used to send me out to get him a pint every lunch hour to which I objected but had to do it. Our job was to check the proofs of the shipping gazette and other publications. I read one copy out loud whilst he checked the other copy for errors, which he marked to be corrected by the printers.

This firm has uniformed messenger boys, whose job was to run to various firms with proofs and plates used in printing. Since it was an outdoor job, I applied for a vacancy and came before the board of directors. They decided that I was more suited to clerical work in the accounts department. Now this was a big room with a parquet floor and desks set around with plenty of space but most of the staff were girls. I didn't care much for them, besides which, I was very shy & very conscious of my working goods, hand-me-down coat, and short trousers, so I insisted on being a messenger boy. This suited me at the time, as I could see all the fascinating things in the windows of the various country agencies, e.g., Canada, America, South America and Africa. I was always fascinated by the display of the various products, such as peaches, apricots, pears, and apples, usually sealed in glass jars of spirit or something. I didn't see much of Australian produce as at that time they only had a small drab building near the mall.

Naturally enough, my dawdling of these errands got me into trouble with the manager and I had to go before the board who had decided if I would not go into the account office, I would have to go.

Looking back, I see I have left out several incidents that have probably helped to shape my life and outlook. E.g., every summer we went on what was called 'the country holiday fund holidays', each school child was issued a pence card each year and he or his parents were expected to make a weekly donation, as much or little as they could afford. Most kids had to put their pocket money in, wages were only 35/- a week. Dad might sometimes get a bit extra by way of commission but living costs were in accordance, e.g., beer was 1 pound a pint. Then in June, those of us who had managed to get a certain amount- I don't know what it was but somehow it always reached it in my case. I have a suspicion that the teachers, who received and signed the cards, put any balance in. They were then boarded out with selected families at either Dover or Petersfield. Petersfield was my favorite place, beautiful woods, and fields on the downs beneath the white house hill – this was cut out of the foil, exposed by the white chalk underneath. Here, we could ramble and do what we pleased, provided we behaved ourselves and came in on time for meals and at dark, which was often not until 10pm. We were of course given a sandwich and allowed to miss dinner, which I did often.

Another incident which affected my outlook:

Grandfather used his front room as a workshop and sat before his bench in front of the windows, making or mending books and shoes. I would sit and watch him as I learnt the techniques. Neither of us ever spoke, from what I remember, as I would settle in his windows and just watch. He would glance up and then go on with his work, I think I was a little scared of him. He was very fond of mussels and at dinner time, he would eat them at his bench. One day, he said nothing and held one out to me, still in the shell. I put it in my mouth and backed slowly away until he couldn't see me and then ran outside our house and spat it out.

Sometime later, not long before he died, he handed me a little brown book called "Astronomy" and said, "read that", so I did. I must have been very young and small because I remember dad coming in, picking me up and taking me into granddad, where he lay in his bed, to say goodbye. I have been interested in Astronomy ever since and it seems that I must have learnt to read at a very early age.

In those days, parents were very keen that their children should be good scholars. Reading and spelling were the number one priority.

But back to the job, after leaving Eyre & Spottiswoode, I got a job with the "Bar-lock" typewriter company. My job was to act as shop boy, getting parts from the store as required by the mechanics. I was given an old typewriter and told to take it to pieces and put it together again. In between time, I certainly took it to pieces but never did get around to putting it together again. The girls in the storeroom were young woman around 19 or 20 years old. They were always trying to call me inside the store, telling me what a nice young-looking boy I was but I was too scared and took good care never to go behind the counter. To avoid the girls at lunchtime, I used to climb to the roof and have my lunch there. I could see the tops of trees in the distance and would think longingly of Petersfield and how lovely it would be to live in the woods there all on my own, away from people and the noisy dirty city.

So, on Thursday when I collected my pay 7/6 (Seven Shillings and Six Pence). Instead of going home, I went to the station and bought a ticket to Richmond, with a vague idea that it was surrounded by woods but when I got out at Richmond, it was starting to get dark and to my terrible disappointment, it wasn't a country village. It turned out to be a big town and a big policeman was on the platform. I didn't know what to do, I had always like our policeman, and we had always got on well with them. I was only a scared little boy of 14 ½, anyway, things solved themselves. He came up and asked me how I was doing and when I couldn't tell him, he took me along to the station, fed me a thick slice of bread with jam and a big mug of tea. The next morning, he took me back to London, where mum met me and took me home. She asked me why I did it and wondered if I thought that I wasn't treated well at home. I just couldn't explain how I longed to get away from all the people in the city, the noise, and the dirt. Dad wouldn't let himself believe that I had run away from home and although he knew the fare to Richmond would have taken some of my wages, insisted that I must have gambled it away. Don't get me wrong, my mother was one of the most fanatically clean women I had ever seen; equaled only by her granddaughter Ruth.

So, on Monday back to the typewriter factory, but this time I was determined to get away differently. During my time as a messenger, I remember seeing a notice in Shaftesbury Avenue, in the window of Shaftesbury office for destitute children. All it showed was a picture of the top of the training ship "Arethusa" and beneath the words "Train for the Navy".

The Shaftesbury trust has vacancies for boys of good character who wish to go to sea. Apply with three-character references within. So, during lunch hour, I went around and obtained an application form. Then I had to get the character references. Mr. Heird, of the typewriter company, gave me one and congratulated me on going to fight for my country (although, this was farthest from my thoughts) and he had the wrong idea. The old boss gave me another and Mr. Clarke, my old teacher, the third.

Dad was the stumbling block. We had always been fairly close, and he didn't altogether like the idea. His uncle, George Honey, had gone to sea, or immigrated, and hadn't been heard from again. I pointed out that I was only going down to the Thames as far as Rotherhithe. Dad was in the Royal Army Medical Corps at St. Thomas's hospital. Will was in the Royal Horse Artillery and Alf was in France with the 2nd rites of London Royal Fusiliers. Jim and Bert, 2 younger brothers, were in the boy scouts.

The scouts' jobs in those early days were to ride around in Lorries when an air raid was on, tell people to take cover and tell people when it was clear, later of course, the sirens were installed.

So, dad signed the papers and off I went after being medically examined by the Shaftesbury people's doctor. This was a very perfunctory affair, consisting of reading a line from a book and seeing that we had no hernias. This would have been about September 1914 because I came out of hospital in

June 1914, got the job with E & S in July and with Barlock in August, just before war was declared.

Chapter Two: Arethusa

We were knitted out with bellbottoms, jumpers, and capes etc., underclothes, nightshirts, books, two of everything. Arriving at Rotherhithe, the big cutter, with 14 boys at the oars awaited us and rowed us out to the Arethusa. Which was anchored out 300 yards. ¼ of a mile eastern was the three decker "Worchester", the training ship for cadets for merchant service officers and ¼ mile ahead the "Warspite", a two decker for delinquent boys.

While we were standing on the gun deck, waiting to be allocated our numbers and quarters, the captain, Commander Martin R.N, came out from the roof, approached and said, "you're an intelligent looking lad, what is your name?". When I told him, he just nodded and said, "I trust you will do well". He was a very big man with one eye and had lost the other at battle of the Nile when the Kitchener's expeditionary were forced to relieve Khartoum.

I was given a hammock and bedding for one mattress, very thin, and one blanket. I was given the number 42 and shown where to sling the hammock on the hooks with my number over them. Mine were over the end of the mess table where we would have our meals. Then we were shown how to hang the hammocks which were composed of heavy canvass with sewn eyelets at head and feet, in these were cords, 12 each end, which were attached to an iron ring at the other end.

We were shown how to lash and stow the hammocks and told we were expected to do this in less than 5 minutes at reveille each morning and put them in the racks. We were only shown it once. The thing to do was to pick a chum who came from the same district and get him to help at first. I was lucky in finding such a chap who also came from Kennington, and we were each other's towny, as if it was called.

But, next morning when "Reveille on Charlie", as it was called blew. Before I had time to move, I found myself sitting in the tub of icy cold water which was always filled and placed at the end of each mess table. Unfortunately for me, I was the nearest hammock to the gangway and as such, was expected to be the first out and away. Anyway, I was the first to get washed and dressed and as a new boy, I was excused this once for not being on time with the hammock in the racks. I had to take it up the upper deck to dry it and the bedding. I realized that complaining would get me nowhere and do no good, so forgot all about it, but guess who was first up and out from then on.

Navy Reveille (Charly)

Charly, Charly lash up your hammock,

And Charly Charly stow it away

Now lash it up Charlie, now lash it up

Charly now lash up your

hammock and stow it away

Charly Charly lash up your hammock

And Charly Charly stow it away

The first day was rather frightening for me at first because the first job was to follow the captain up the rigging, starboard side, out over the hanging shrouds, across the foretop platform and down the portside to the deck. We new chums were excused from the hanging shrouds but went through the lubber's hole.

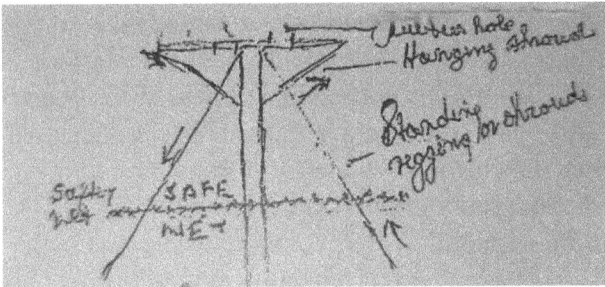

The captain, who must have been in his fifties, led the way and we followed with only our trousers rolled to the knee and a singlet, bare feet too. This was the first exercise every morning, winter and summer. Even when the shrouds were covered in ice, although then we were allowed more time. Then came physical jerks and at 7:30 prayers on the after deck. Followed by breakfast, which consisted of burgoo (porridge with bread, butter and jam, meat of some kind, usually fried. Then the watches were mustered into their respective tops. Foretop, Forecastle and Quarterdeck. I was in the Foretop squad, these were sent to their respective part of the ship, except us new boys, we were sent to the after deck below, which was used as a schoolroom.

There were two school masters, the senior Evans and Mr Mcloumick. Mr. Evans set us all a paper in dictation and arithmetic and to my disgrace, I funked out on the arithmetic. He called me aside and asked, was I not the boy who topped the 1913 Polytechnic exams. I said I was, he dressed me down and gave me a week to pass an exam. I'm glad to say that two days later, I was able to go to him and ask for the exam, which I passed easily and was promoted to the senior class. This class together with the advanced navy class met ashore in the afternoon's schoolrooms on the jetty. In the mornings, we had to learn to box the compass both ways. This consisted of repeating aloud the points of the compass. Starting first at North, Eastwards around and back to North and then reverse. This we had to memorize and be able to repeat at short notice at any moment. I earned a penny from Mr. Ward for being the first to do so.

Boxing the Compass

North, North by East, Northeast by North, Northeast

Northeast by East, East Northeast, East by North, East.

East by South, East Southeast, Southeast by East,

Southeast, Southeast by South, South Southeast,

South by East, South.

South by West, South Southwest, Southwest by South,

Southwest, Southwest by West, Southwest by South

Southwest, Southwest by West, West Southwest,

West by South, West.

West by North, West Northwest, Northwest by West,

Northwest, Northwest by North, North Northwest, North by West, North.

(We write it like this, in reverse this time)

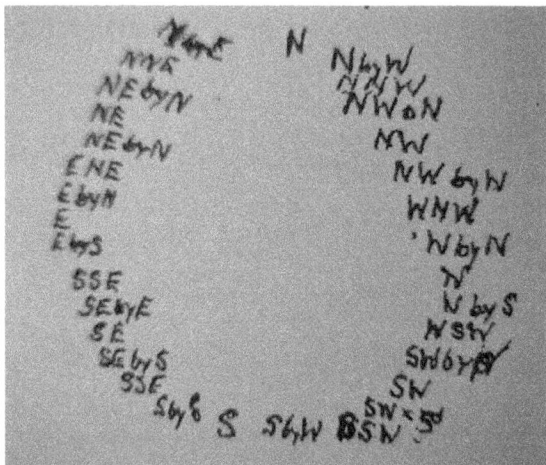

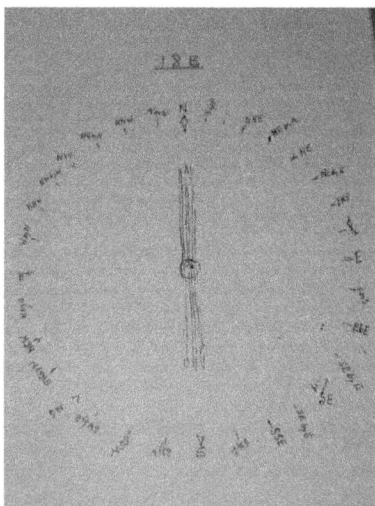

After an hour of this, we had to learn the knot. This was taken by Mr. Downs, a long rope was stretched at waist height along the mess deck and on it, hung two thinner lines or rather one line draped over the rope. One for each boy and on this we learned the different hitches, close hitch, half hitch, rolling hitch, reef knot, granny knot, timber hitch etc.; one hour on that, then to knots and splice with separate pieces of rope.

Short splice, long splice, wall knot, brown knot, eye splice, Turk's head, which is made by a wall and a brown and follow the ends round and as on. Mr. Downs would walk along the line of boys with a manrope, a mistake or idle talk and down would come the manrope. This was later changed to a round, feather plaited thong called a "Toby", which stung more but done no real damage. Our teachers were hard bitten old navy seals, chief petty officers, seconded to us from the reserve and given acting rank of Lieutenant. Our second in command liked to throw his weight about, a sadistic B – who was hated by the boys and disliked by the instructors-but more of him later.

Being in the senior class, I only did the rope knotting and splicing in the mornings and as soon as I was proficient in this, I was excused further instruction and went with my senior classmates on ship side work, which consisted of constant repair to rigging, fittings, care of the boats etc.

This occasionally arose some jealousy among the other new boys and some of the older ones who had not managed to get beyond the first class and still had to go to school. I suffered accordingly as I was small and slight and no match for the bigger boys. There was only one way out and that was to increase my standing so that I would have some authority. To that end I volunteered to join the first aid class, ran by Mr. Jones sick berth attendant. Then a peculiar thing happened, one day one of the boys fell from the foretop through the net and crashed onto the bitts, these are solid wooden blocks 3ft high and 15" square set around the mast in a square, with fife rail in between, these held the belaying pins to which the various ropes and halyard are bent. His back was broken, he was taken ashore, and we saw him no more.

The senior and advanced navy master were immediately put to work making a new net and no one was allowed aloft until it was finished. Playing tag with my mate a few days later, after the new net had been strung, running out around the monkey topsail yard, and grabbing for the shroud at the far end, I missed and hit the new net, mostly with my face. The new net was of course tarred and set off an allergy, causing me to come up with a terrible rash all over my face, arms, and legs. I was taken to the sickbay and kept there for a fortnight. Every two hours, I had to bathe my face, arms, and legs in oatmeal water. The arms and legs cleared very quickly, the face took longer, but meanwhile, I was swatting up on first aid. Mr. Jones tried me out by throwing questions at me whenever he thought of a new one. In consequence, I came top in the exam, was given my certificate and alas made a second-class petty officer boy. From that moment, the bullying stopped, and I began to enjoy the work. Also, in the senior class, we had to learn all about boats and boat work, but the rank carried responsibilities too since I now had to take my share of duties with the other petty officer boys. This was to act as quarter master on the gangway together with the Officer of the Watch and to act as coxswain of the duty boats crew. The duty boat being a gig, this meant being called away from whatever I was doing, round up the crew and man the gig for whoever was going ashore, or to bring anyone from the shore. We often did nothing else but pull the boat back and forth during our hour of duty, still I liked this part best.

The Arethusa, Worchester and Warspite were of course often used as targets by the Zeppelins who used the Thames as a guide on their way to London. They never managed to hit any of the ships, although, on the night which the Zepp was brought down just across the river in Essex. One bomb just missed our bowsprit by about 30 ft. It was a bright moonlight night, and we were all up on deck in our night shirts and saw the bomb fall, then later watched the airship break in half and fall in flames to the ground. To us it was just like a play and wasn't real, so we weren't anyways scared.

At the end of the year, I passed into the advanced navigation class, and I entered for the seamanship examination. We entered in pairs, my towny and I, unfortunately he wasn't as good as he should have been. I only picked him because he was my towny, not because he was any champion at seamanship. We were given 9ft of rope and with it we had to make in it 4 splices and 4 knots if I remember rightly. I think it was eye splice, back splice, short splice, and long splice. The knots were the wall and crown, Turk's head and I have forgotten the fourth knot but the wall + crown and Turk's head were of course embodied in the one knot and was used to finish one end. Anyway, we came only 4th in seamanship, and I was made a first-class petty officer boy and my towny was made a second class. Then came the exams in semaphore and morse. I and one other boy were running neck to neck, the prize was a telescope.

Unfortunately for me, the examining officer was Lt. Smith, who always made me nervous as he seemed to dislike me for some reason. I never fathomed and while I did well in the semaphore, when it came to the morse, I was unable to read it as quickly as he sent it and I believe he made it faster for me than the other chap and he got the telescope. I wasn't all that disappointed, as the captain was there, he patted me on the shoulder and said that I had done very well, considering that the other lad was older than me and had 12 months more service. In fact, he left for Chatham the following day.

I was made a Chief Petty Officer boy and became captain of the foretop in the port hatch. I also became coxswain of the captain's gig, a small boat, pulled by four boys which was kept scrupulously clean, scrubbed, and painted with white cotton lanyards fitted to the tiller head, it was white with blue stripes around the rubbing strake. Whenever the captain went ashore – or his wife – who lived on board, this is the boat that they used and the call would go out, "away captain's gig". I and the four crew would have to drop everything and man the gig, which was always kept riding on a line from the end of the boom. On the call, we would run out along the boom, drop the line to the boat and bring it to the gangway platform. This practice was discontinued after the first Christmas, as it was risky and if you fell in the water, the chances were you would be swept under the platform and drowned.

The advanced navy class was concerned with boat sailing, logarithms, chart reading and principle of navigation and ship steering. Whenever possible, we would be given the opportunity aboard one of the big branch line cargo ships, coming up or down the Thames, to try our hand at the wheel. It was not for very long, needless to say, as the Thames is a tricky river and flows very fast on an outgoing tide but the reach which we were in was very wide and fairly long. The ships were all named after the tree branches, e.g., Elm branch, Oak branch etc.

We were allowed ashore on Sunday afternoons, but were not supposed to go beyond certain limits, but of course being boys, they were just the places we liked the best. One of these was a clay quarry, we used to go there and have great fun pushing the trucks used to take the clay to the riverside, up and down the lines. This came to a sudden end one Sunday, when we were pushing a truck loaded with clay down the rails towards the river, intending to switch it to another line, the trouble was, after getting it started, it gathered speed and we couldn't stop it and before we could get to the points to sidetrack it, it got there first and went straight down to the end of the jetty. It went up and over the ramp, which tilted in the air and into the river. We, of course, disowned all knowledge and promptly decamped. No one had seen us so we got off scot free, had we been caught, it would have meant twelve clubs with the cane on the buttocks, stretched over the gymnasium horse and dismissal from the ship.

I only saw one boy punished this way, it was a nasty experience and would not be tolerated today. The boy was stretched across the horse and held down by four senior boys, one on each limb. Then Mr. Smith took a 6ft cane, 3/4" thick, whistled it through the air and then brought it down with all his force on the boy's buttocks. He was brought to the sick bay afterwards while I was there and he had twelve great welts across his bottom, the trousers had saved the skin from being broken and he was not excused duty but behind Smiths back, Mr.

Collins – the next senior officer – sent him down to the lower deck to perform light duties of some kind. I think that was the day I really felt hate for Smith and the day was to come when I would be responsible for his dismissal.

We boys were always hungry, although fed well enough, and so one Sunday, No. 48 and myself, went ashore for a long walk and came across a field of turnips, there was a path across the fields and this path skirted along the wood at the far end. At this point, we decided to have a feed of turnips, we were busily chowing away when I happened to look up and saw the captain's cap just appearing over the river at the far end of the field. His wife was with him and as we jumped up, he saw us and yelled to us to stand fast, we knew he wasn't close enough to identify us, he could only know that he'd seen two boys in uniform.

We promptly dived into the wood. We scrambled up the hill and lay down in the bracken. The skipper came through the wood but couldn't see us and then went his way. We got up and walked through a spinney, we came out amongst rows and rows of raspberries, black and white currants, and strawberries. Boy! Did we have a feed; we took care not to damage anything but 48, who wasn't all that bright, insisted on filling a handkerchief. I pointed out that Mr. Collins was the officer at the watch, and he would never get past him. He was confident that he could, so when we got to the peer, I got well up in the bows of the big cutter and 48 sat on one of the thwarts and of course, all the other boys crowded in until we were loaded. When we got to the gangway, I was fist out and up the ladder and reported myself aboard, the others followed one by one. 48 had put his handkerchief of strawberries down inside his jumper and in the crush of boys, they got squashed. Of course, Jumper (Mr. Collins) spotted the stash. "No. 48 in the after deck at the double", and poor old 48 had to go inside the after deck and wait. When all the boys had reported in, Jumper went in to the after deck. "No. 48, what's that in your jumper?", "strawberries, Sir" No. 48 replied. "Where did you get them?", Jumper asked. "A farmer gave them to me Sir".

Now Jumper was very strict but also very understanding of boys, so he didn't ask which farmer or where, as he had a shrewd idea about it, so all he said was, "bend over, 6 cuts with the toby", which he duly applied and then, "get yourself below, clean yourself up and don't be such a bloody fool again".

He knew that I had been ashore with 48 but all he said to me when I reported to the gangway for quartermasters' duty at 6pm was, "you like strawberries 42?", I said, "not much, Sir", and that was particularly enough, I don't go much on strawberries either, even now.

On another occasion, a local farmer caught some of the boys red-handed, he didn't prosecute but asked the boys whether they got fruit onboard, we didn't, and they told him so. So, he let them go and see they did get some, sure enough the following Tuesday, he hauled the gig and brought a sack of apples and told the captain Marten that they were specially for the boys and from then on through, a sack of apples came aboard each week. Otherwise, the only fruit we got was what our parents sent us in parcels from home, this was applied to cake and biscuits as well.

Harking back to the turnip episode, we went in fear and trembling when we got back aboard for, we were afraid that it was just possible for the captains wife to have recognized us as Arethusa boys as we wore black silks and white lanyards around our collars, whereas the Warspite boys didn't, as far as I knew. If she did know, she never let on, because at prayers in the afterdeck that Sunday night, the skipper asked that if the boys he had seen in a turnip field that afternoon were Arethusa boys, he expected them to come forward and honestly own up to being out of bounds. I think that he really believed that we would, as he was very proud of our reputation and for that very reason, we couldn't admit it. After a while, he looked around and said, "I'm very glad, it must have been some of the Warspite lads".

Then came the episode that finished Mr. Smith. He was a very arrogant type, very puffed with his own importance, although, he was only a 2nd lieutenant on the reserve list who had been passed over for promotion and was only acting as a full lieutenant for training purposes.

This particular day, I was duty coxswain of the duty gig, and we were pulled away to pull ashore to bring Mr. Kendrick, the schoolmaster, back to the ship. It was wintertime and we were wearing boots and socks, this applied only to the gigs crew. The captain issued strict orders that the moment the bell tolled for prayers at 7pm, every boy, no matter what his duties, was to drop everything and go straight to the afterdeck.

As we came to the gig, the bell tolled for prayers, normally, we would have gone below and removed our boots and socks with our trousers rolled to our knees and then gone up, but in lieu of the captains' orders, I told my crew to repair after the quarter deck, led them there and took my place at their head. Smith was conducting the service and as we marched in, gave me a glare. At the end of the service, he gave the order, "gigs crew stand fast, ships company right and left turn dismiss". So, we were left standing by ourselves. Smith strolled over with both hands in his trouser pockets, planted himself in front of me and said, "you know the order about boots and shoes to be removed when you come aboard", I said "yes, sir", he said "crew, dismiss" and then he said to me "you'd countermand my orders would you?" and lifting his hand, drew it back and with all his might, smacked me across the left side of my head, knocking me into the scupper and almost unconscious, then walked back to his cabin.

I got to my feet, clasping my hand to my ear and literally staggered out to the gangway. Mr. Ward was a duty officer, he grabbed me by the arm and asked me what was wrong. I couldn't answer so he took me below and into Jumper's cabin and made me sit down. Jumper wanted to know what had happened and when I told him, he looked at Ward and said the captain must know about this. Then he said to me that next Sunday I was to take my place at the end of the line of the captain's request men.

This was an institution of the captain's, whereby any boy could, after prayers, go to the captain's cabin and make any request direct to him, even if he only wanted to wish him well. There were always boys who went to see him on Sunday, and I tagged along, the last in the line, as instructed. Smith was on his weekend off and was not present. No officer was allowed to strike a boy except with a toby or manrope and this was limited also, so when the skipper asked me what he could do for me, Jumper stepped in and explained I was there at his directions and told me to tell the captain exactly what had happened. I told him and he said, "why didn't you take your shoes and socks off when you came aboard?", I explained that the bell was tolling as we tied up the gig and by the time we reached the gangway, we were the only ones not in the afterdeck and that in lieu of his own strict orders, I ordered the crew into the afterdeck". All he said was "quite right, you may go", and I left. On Monday when Smith came around, all the officers were called to the captain's quarters, where I understand that Smith was told of the allegations against him, he tried to bluster his way out of it and accused me of needing stricter discipline. This was promptly denied by all the other officers. Mr. Ward said he had been a duty officer and had heard Mr. Smith and the blow and said I was quite dazed when I staggered out to the gangway.

The upshot of all this was that Mr. Smith was then seen going ashore with all of his gear and we didn't see him on the ship again.

As a chief petty officer boy, I had full control of the foretop crew, both post and starboard watches under Lt. Cotton and I had always the day duty of the captain of the duty gig and I was for the rest of my stay aboard, fulltime coxswain of the captains gig – which by the way, was a whaler sharp at both ends, a bit longer than the duty gig-, and each morning we took it out for a run instead of going over the masthead. This served a double purpose, as if a boy fell overboard, we were in position to pick him up. None ever did in my time, although we were always hoping one would, so we could have got the job of picking him up.

It was on one of these mornings that I saw a large bundle of something floating out in the stream, we raced the boat back to the landing stage. I ran up the gangway and reported to Mr. Mainwazing, who had replaced Mr. Ward who was called up for active duty and told him that I would take the duty gig and investigate. He was new and just nodded so my crew and I took the duty gig and pulled out after the bundle, which was slowly floating down the stream, as the tide had just turned. I hooked it with the boat hook and tied it to the landing stage, it turned out to be a corpse and the captain was a bit annoyed as it meant a coroner's inquest and of course the attendance of an officer to explain the circumstances of its finding. I should explain here that anything floating down the river was investigated as to its value. Timber and sometimes boxes, which might contain anything from fruit to tins of milk or fruit etc. and all sorts of odds and ends that could prove useful, timber especially.

But to get back to the job, myself and two other petty officer boys were halfway up the foretop port shrouds, repairing ratlines, these are the series of footropes fastened across the shrouds and act as a ladder. Tommy Cotton was just below us on the main deck putting a Turks head on a new gangway man rope. One of the boys said, "old Tommy's a deaf old bastard", Tommy looked up and said, "Tommy mightn't be such a deaf old bastard as you think". We were very fond of old Tommy, he was one of the old schools of square riggers, he had served in the navy from boyhood in the time when it was still mostly sail and steam. He had been around the hour both ways and was a wonderful teacher, teaching by example, rather than by book. He had quite a fund of anecdotes of life in the navy in the old days, the trouble was to get him going, when he did, it always pointed a moral of some kind and explained why things were done a certain way.

Mr. Harley, the advanced navy class teacher was another of the older school, not as old as Mr. Cotton, he nevertheless had a fund of stories which always showed up some point or reason that was relevant to the teaching. On Friday afternoons, before returning to the ship, at 3pm, he would read from a storybook such as Huckleberry Finn or Mr. Midshipman Easy. On Saturdays after cleaning down decks and generally tidying up the afternoons were allocated to two or three different types of sports. Football ashore in the playing field, boat pulling, or a walking party. I got enough boat pulling through the week as well as on Saturdays, I didn't like football, so I chose the walking party. This was conducted by Mr. Kendrick, who was by this time, the only school master. Mr. Evans having been recalled for active duty with the fleet. I used to look forward to these walks through the fields and woods, for this part of Kent was very beautiful and Mr. Kendrick was a very kind old gentleman who would sometimes buy us fruit.

Unfortunately, it was through him that we had a very narrow escape from disaster. It happened this way. It was a rigid custom that when an officer entered the boat, he was offered the tiller by the coxswain. At the time of this incident, I was coxswain of the duty gig, and the Thames was in flood with a strong outgoing tide, easily 8 to 10 knots. In consequence when pulling the gig ship to shore or vice versa, instead of travelling straight across, we had to pull upstream and pull hard. If the tide had been coming in, we would have had to pull downstream, so that between the tide and the oars one would travel almost straight across and just nose gently onto the jetty or the ship, as the case might be. Now downstream from our jetty about ¼ mile, almost opposite the Worchester, was an old wharf on piles that jutted out to the river; the river used to swirl in and around these piles setting up whirlpools and back currants. A very dangerous hazard to anyone ignorant of its dangers and we had been warned never to get near it as we would certainly be swamped and almost certainly drowned.

On this occasion Mr. Kendrick who had been ashore all morning, signaled from the jetty about 2pm to come aboard. I called my crew, and we took the gig and jumper Collins, who, thank the lord, was the duty officer on the gangway. He warned me to pull well upstream as the currant was very strong. This I did and it took very hard pulling by the four boys of the crew and with the tiller hand over to get across to the jetty. It was only 30 yards, but we had to pull twice the distance upstream to make it, and actually, I doubt if we travelled upstream more than a few yards, as we really travelled crab fashion (see diagram).

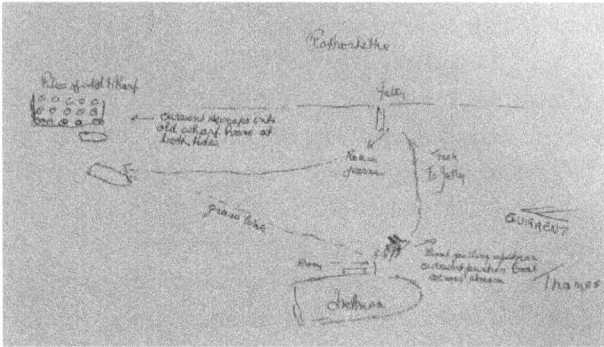

When Mr. Kendrick got into the boat, I offered him the tiller which he took, and I double banked the stroke oar. As we cleared over the jetty, Mr. Kendrick put the tiller amidships apparently thinking we would go straight across, but of course the currant immediately began to sweep us downstream. Mr. Collins was watching and through a megaphone shouted to pull upstream. Mr. Kendrick was quite bewildered and obviously didn't know what to do. I pushed him aside, put the helm hard over and told him to hold it there, then I got back on the stroke oar and told the boys to pull like hell, putting all my own weight on the stroke oar.

We were rapidly swept towards the wharf as the rudder was having practically no effect. Luckily, Jumper Collins realized what had happened, had all hands-on deck and the big cutter had lowered in no time and attached to a grass line and himself in the cutter let it sweep down towards us. Meanwhile, he was urging us to pull like hell and just as it looked as if we were going under the piles, the cutter came level and I was able to let go of the oar, grab the cutters gunwale, and then the rope Mr. Collins gave me and go forward and fasten it to the bow ring.

While this was going on, the 480 boys onboard had carried the grass line through the upper deck port from the end of the boom and manned it right along the deck. As soon as we were made fast to the stern of the cutter, Jumper raised his hand high, the signal for the boys onboard to start pulling and only just in time. I could have touched the piles of the old wharf, but with the 480 boys running that coin line up the deck, it was like being towed by a motorboat, for the boys just held the rope and ran with up the deck.

As the first boys reached the forecastle, they would run back and grab the rope where it came through the port and off again. It's the fastest trip in a no engine boat I have ever had. It is thanks to the watchfulness, prompt action and initiative of Jumper Collins that I am able to write this today. The captain congratulated us on the tremendous effort we had made and not panic, but actually, there was no time to panic or be afraid, we had to pull too hard to keep away from those piles to think of anything else; but the order went out, from that time on, the tiller was offered to no-one except a seaman officer.

The big cutter shipped 16 oars but usually only used 14. The second big cutter was used for training in boat sailing on the river. We had had a tender, the "Chichester", which had been used for sea going training. She was ketch rigged but the naval chiefs stopped us using her because of the war. She used to run round to Harwick and bring back stores, but with our younger instructors being called to active service there were not enough officers to take her.

Then came the time for me to leave "Arethusa" and report to the depot at Chatham. I had been on the training ship for two years, had I not done so well there I would have been sent off as soon as I reached 15 1/2; as it was, I had passed all exams for Boy as 1st class and would go to Chatham as one.

I had to remove my badges but was checked over to see that I had a full kit. Peculiarly, except for the very cursory exam when I first joined, we had never had a medical exam, but nobody expected any difficulty, all I was told, was, that I would be expected to swim three lengths of the pool before my rating as a 1st class boy would be confirmed and this was no problem. On arrival at Chatham, I was taken to the reporting officer who confirmed that I was signed in for 12 or 21 years, but I was then told that my time didn't start until I was 18 years old. This meant that I had served from August 1914 to September 1916 for free and would continue to do so for another 1 ½ years until I had reached 18 in March 1918. I was asked if I understood this and I said "yes", then I was sent to fleet surgeon Reed for a thorough medical check. He started with the eyes, first left then the right eye. Then he told me that I had stigmatism in the right eye, and he thought that I would probably grow out of it. There was then confab with other officers and it was decided that I would be seconded to the merchant service for a period of 6 months, when I was to report back to fleet surgeon Reed. In the meantime, I was to report back to the Arethusa and await arrangements for me to be sent to London and aboard a ship.

When I arrived back on the "Arethusa" there was a certain amount of consternation. I hadn't known that the Shaftesbury Trust paid £50 for every boy who was fully trained and accepted. In this instance, they wouldn't get the £50 for another six months.

The captain was very brusque with me and asked me if I had purposely failed, when I said I'd never even thought of such a thing, he grunted and said that it was a terrible thing to have let the side down, just as if it was my fault. Then he asked me if I would like to stay aboard and train as a shipwright. I would have liked this and it's really what I should have done, but fleet surgeon Reed had said I was to go into the Merchant Service for six months and I stuck to this. There was nothing they could really do about it, unless I agreed to stay aboard, which I refused to do. Had they not adopted such a bullying manner, I would have agreed to stay aboard and train as a shipwright, as it was, I got my back up and stuck to the fleet surgeon's instruction.

I was then instructed to go to London and report to Captain Evans, who would arrange for me to be placed aboard a suitable ship. It was fairly late when I arrived at Captain Evans, and he was very disgruntled and said some very nasty things about Commander Martin. He obviously wasn't keen on having to get me booked in for the night, so I pointed out that I only lived a train ride away and after I satisfied him that I would turn up at 9 am the next morning, he gave me the tram fare and I went home. At home of course, I had to tell mum and dad what it was all about, and dad said I must take after his uncle George who had gone to sea and they hadn't heard from him since.

CHAPTER 3: SS PORT CAMPBELL

Next morning, I duly reported to Captain Evans, and he took me round to the shipping masters office where I was duly signed on to the SS Port Campbell due to sail the following day. I was duly warned to be ready at 8am the next morning at the Victoria + Albert docks with one mattress, seaboots, oilskins, plate, knife, fork, spoon and at least one blanket; these captain Evans told me to get from him the next morning at the ships side and I was told that the ship was sailing to Australia via New York to Freemantle, Adelaide, Melbourne and Sydney, thence to New Zealand and back home, so I went home that day really excited, as were mum and dad when I told them, but they weren't so bright next morning when I had to get up early to get to the docks on time. Mum wanted to come and see me off, but I wiped that one, no tearful farewells for me.

The trouble was that "Aboukir", "Hogue", and "Greasy", three cruisers had been sunk, one after the other by the same "LL" boat and although nothing had been said, the thought was in all our minds, that it could happen to us, but it didn't really mean much to me. I somehow knew that nothing would happen to me, and mum had always said that I'd never drown, although I might get hung. She did have some psychic ability, and this stood her in good stead later on.

So, we sailed just as the tide turned to run out and as we passed the Arethusa on the Rotherhithe reach, I leapt onto the No. 4 hatch and semaphored to the Arethusa to let the boys know I was there, and that's where my troubles began.

I didn't realise that at that time, there was a great deal of animosity between naval and merchant personnel, I was navy and proud of it at the time. The coxswain was a Liverpool Irishman, a small wiry man, cunning as they come and with a deep hatred of the Navy and navy men. His son was the ships carpenter "Chips" as he was known and a naval reservist, and he was on 48 hours standby. This meant that if he went ashore, he had to report to the nearest Naval Depot, so he didn't go ashore. He was a nice chap, not like his father, and he and I became quite friendly, but he was taciturn and said very little. He did tell me to take care of his father, as he was very bitter about something to do with the navy.

However, the Port Campbell was a singles crew ship of about 4,000 tons, an ex-member of the "Tyser Line", commandered from the Germans at the outbreak of the war and given to the Cunard freighter fleet which sailed as the "Commonwealth and Dominion Line", now called the "Port" line. They were all named after a port in Australia and New Zealand. Port Campbell, Port Hacking, Port Lyttleton, etc. and they traded between America to Australia and New Zealand.

I got a terrible shock when I saw the accommodation, we were quartered in the fo'c's'le, stokers on the port side, seaman on the starboard side and there was only the chain locker in between us and the stem of the ship, thus, so when the ship was underway there would be the noise of the anchor chains rattling against the bulkhead together with the rushing sound of the sea, our quarters would be about 18ft long by about 8ft wide at the widest part, narrowing towards the stem, there were two tiers of three bunks against the ships side, with two tiers of two bunk beds on the bulkhead side. In between was a table long and narrow which slid up and down on two square posts and except at mealtimes was kept pegged up near the deck head out of the way. It was brought down at mealtimes and there was just enough room to sit on the lower bunks and get your knees under the tables. This sort of accommodation would not be tolerated today. All personnel gear was kept in your kit bag or box under the lower bunks; just left of our quarters there were two cabins, one for the bosun + lamp trimmer and one for the carpenter + donkeyman. Their quarters weren't much better, except they had a certain amount of privacy.

So, we proceeded to sea, and of course when we got out into the channel and struck the rough seas, I became seasick, as did the ships boy named Vesey. I don't know what he did, but the mate called me up to the bridge, gave me a bucket and scrubber and told me to scrub the bridge. This I did for the next three days in between bouts of violent sickness; all I could eat was ships biscuit and drink coffee. The mate made sure I did, I thought it was terrible at the time and I thought that he was a sadist, but looking back, I can see that he was doing the best thing for me, as I was never sick again. The biscuit and coffee kept me alive and gave my stomach something to work on. I would have been glad to be sunk by a LL boat, but we sighted nothing, anyway we were an empty ship with ballast only, and if a LL boat had seen us, he would, at that stage, probably have saved his torpedoes for something more worthwhile. Also, at that time they seemed to look more for warships.

Here I should point out that I was signed on as an extra as I was still Navy personnel, and directly under the care of the mate (Mr. Williams). He was held responsible for my care and upkeep and was supposed to teach me to steer and navigate. All he ever did was give me an hour steering once. The rumors were that a gun and guns crew were to be acquired at New York and that I would then be placed with them, but nothing came of this. DATA (Do As Time Allows)

After the first three days we ran out of bad weather, and it was wonderful. As far as the eye could see nothing but water, great heaving rollers, which would lift the ship, first under the bow, which would rise up and up until you'd be looking straight up into the sky, or so it seemed. Then the bow would sink down and, the stern would rise, and you would be looking straight into what looked like a great mountain of water rolling majestically down on you. Suddenly, you'd realise how small the ship really was and what a little pygmy you really were, and you'd feel a terrible awe. At least I did, but then you would eventually get used to it, and begin to really enjoy yourself, only there was always the bosun ready for some brass work to polish or woodwork to scrub although you knew it was a waste of time, as the brass would be mildewed again, and the woodwork salted up again the next day.

Except for the four quarter masters the other three seaman were on daywork. That is from 6 – 8am then 8:30am to 12 noon, 1pm -4pm. Of course, we were liable at any time, if any necessity arose, to be called out. On Sundays we only had to wash down the deck and were free the rest of the day to wash our clothes, or ourselves, if necessary, you simply stripped off and used the deck hose with some water soap.

As it was the same routine every day, it became very boring after a while, especially so after we left New York after a five-day crossing, we berthed on the Brooklyn side near the Brooklyn bridge. The thing that caught my eye, more than the Statue of Liberty was a tremendous advertising sign "UNEEDA BISCUIT", it must have been longer than our ship and proportionally high, and to me it seemed to dominate the harbor. Everything was strange and foreign at first, and it was almost surprising that the people spoke English, but the shop keepers were courteous enough, although hard to understand at times; I didn't at that time realise New York was a hot patch of mixed races.

It was very cold, snow everywhere, and ashore one night, Vesey, -the ships boy-, and I, had the astonishing experience of watching firemen trying to put out a fire in a 10-story building on 42 street, have the water from their hoses turn to ice as it ran down the face of the building. What struck us most was the crowd of people who all seemed to be in a frantic hurry. We were pushed and jostled this way and that, and very soon got fed up, and after buying some fruit, which was very cheap, we made our way back to the ship. This was the beginning of the 1916-17 winter, one of the worst on record. We of course didn't realise this at the time and since I knew that Aunty Drew, as we called her, had gone to America and ran a hotel with her brother, at a place called I believe, Peckville, or similar name, in Pennsylvania.

Now we were berthed at the Brooklyn railway yards and there were long strings of large railway vans stationed in the yard, and right opposite our berth was a string of big vans labelled, I think, "The Ohio and Pennsylvania Railroad". Vesey and I discussed the matter of jumping ship, going to Peckville and looking up Aunty Drew. We thought we may be able to ride horse, round up Indians and generally have a good time. So, the night before we were to sail, we sneaked ashore – there was no security of any kind in America at this stage, I don't think it was thought of, certainly we had no guards on the ship and of course, America was neutral.

Anyway, we had dived across the lines and dived into one of these vans, which had a few bundles of hides in it and settled ourselves down for a ride to Pennsylvania. Certainly, there was no security as we know it today, but there were railway yard police, called "Bulls" here, and luckily for us, one of them spotted us climbing into the van and the next thing we knew, was a bull voice ordering us to come out and no shenanigans. We very meekly crawled out and stood shivering, while he gave us a lecture, and pointed out that, had he not stopped us, we would have been frozen stiff by morning, let alone by the time we reached Pennsylvania. Naturally he was Irish and after the lecture he gave us a light kick in the behind and ushered us back to the ship. Luckily no one aboard was any the wiser about our escapade since, had it become known, we would not have been allowed ashore again.

We left New York the next morning and steamed Southeast. The cold weather was left behind and the days became warm and sunny. Then we saw our first porpoises, a great school of them, stretching for miles across our bows, but they soon left us behind for we could only do 10 knots. Then came the flying fish who could glide for yards before hitting the water, quite a number would come aboard during the night as we were loaded to Plimsoll & Louis in the water, the mate Mr. Williams used to go round first light, pick up the ones who came aboard and have them for breakfast.

At New York we had loaded up with all sorts of goods for the Australian market, there were huge boxes of Nestles chocolates, Café au Lait, Malted milk powder also cases and cases of various foodstuffs. Right at the bottom of the ship were stowed an immense lot of iron bars and plates. The ship had four holds with two decks between the upper deck and the bottom. One was called the tween deck and the other the shelter deck, she was really a hollow box with the engine room and bunkers in the center.

I have made this sketch so that the narrative may be more readily understood in view of what happened later. The fine weather held good until the crossing of the equator, the mate told Vesey to watch closely and told him that he might see the line and feel the bump as we went over it. He didn't try that one on me, probably realizing that my training would have told me different, however, that day was declared a holiday and the seaman prepared to hold the usual ceremony.

Since Vesey and I were the only ones who hadn't crossed the line before, we were of course the victims, we were seized and convicted of the usual crime of trespassing in Neptune's domain without proper authority and without paying a penalty. The carpenter had made a huge wooden razor and we were held down on a stool while a whitewash brush was used to plaster our face and head with a mixture of whitewash made fairly thick, then we were shaved with the wooden razor and then the deck hose was turned on us. I took it as quietly as possible since I knew that to make a fuss would only make matters worse and they sure gave me works, venting their dislikes of the navy onto me, but as I took it in good part, although they nearly chocked me and came close to drowning me, so much so that the mate called a halt, and of course the man on the horse was the coxswain.

From that time on the crew, with the exception of the coxswain and one Australian named Prendergast, became very friendly to me, and the big swede Kruk – pronounced crook -, took me under his wing and declared that anyone who tried to hurt – Barney – as he called me, would have to reckon with him and as he was easily the biggest and strongest man abord, nobody argued the point.

So, we continued on our way across the South Atlantic and saw nothing, except once a large square rigged sailing ship, which Kruk said was probably the "Pamin", carrying wheat from Australia round to Talmouth, she was a beautiful site with all sail set, as the wind was light, we didn't speak to her as she was too far away. The calm weather continued until we were almost up to the Cape of Good Hope which we saw away on the horizon as a dark cloud, the weather had turned colder and rougher as we made the turn to N.E and we were now in the 40° area, known as the roaring 40's because the seas in these latitudes travel unbroken right round the globe.

It was here that I had my second round with the coxswain, who had been hounding me whenever he could, although, strictly speaking, I was directly responsible to the mate, Kruk was on the wheel and the coxswain directed me to get a chipping hammer and scraper, go aft and scrape the paint off the flag staff and in a loud voice, ordered me to be very careful and not fall overboard.

- I forgot to mention that my first round with him had been when he had sent me to paint the chain plates – plates on the deck which took the rub of the rudder chains which ran along the after deck to the quadrant in the after wheelhouse, we were being chased by huge mountains of water, waves as high as our funnel and breaking at the top. I had commenced painting when the stern dropped down, I looked up and there towering over the stern and looking a mile high, was the biggest wave I ever saw bearing down on us and just beginning to break. I was scared almost to death, dropped the paint pot and ran for the cover of the alley way, of course the paint spilt, the stern rose, and the wave passed over us, breaking over the deck and out through the scuppers. It's just possible that I could have been washed overboard, but unlikely. I certainly would have been washed off my feet and thoroughly soaked, but for running for the alleyway.

However, the coxswain had no sympathy for a badly scared boy and berated me soundly and called me a lazy good for nothing naval bastard etc., to which I foolishly replied that he was the biggest bastard on the ship, he told me to get to work and clean up the paint on the deck with Suji holystone, then finish painting the chain plates and not to knock off until I finished. Well, I cleaned the paint off the deck, but the Kruk came off watch and did the plates for me, cuffing me round the head for being scared of a wave. -

So, we came to the second round. I knew that one didn't need a chipping hammer to clean the plate from a wooden flagstaff, but I had to climb on the after rail to get at it, hold it with one hand to save it from falling overboard and work with the others. I tried a hit with the hammer, in case the staff was iron, it wasn't and then the coxswain came round the wheelhouse "I've got you now, you bloody bastard" but I raised the chipping hammer and told him I'd split his skull if he laid a finger on me, he saw the light, told me he'd get me some other time.

I told Kruk about it and said I'd go to the mate, but he said not to do that, leave it to him, he'd fix it.

A few days later, we'd run into a fairly calm patch and Kruk was up at the crossbeam of the fore, getting a strap ready for a block, this strap was of wire rope, and he was using a steel marlinspike. Just then the bosun stopped and looked up, the spike, point first, fell and just cleared his nose. Had he not stopped it, it would have gone through his skull,

Kruk looked down "sorry boss', it slipped through my fingers", the bosun went white as a ghost, said nothing, and went below.

Kruk said to me afterwards that would teach the bastard a lesson, but to watch my step and leave the ship was the first chance I got.

CHAPTER FOUR: FREEMANTLE TO ADELAIDE

After 46 days at sea, without meeting another ship, except the Pamin, we arrived in Freemantle.

There was one incident just after leaving there, the chief steward, who was responsible for cabin stores, had bought a few boxes of apples and these were handles by the stevedores, who under the watchful eye of the chief took them down and stored them in the Lazavet, which was under the after wheelhouse, but the chief didn't know that Kruk had got into the Lazavet to a door leading into the hold forward and had fastened a porthole back so that it was held in the open position by a box of the apples. On the run, from Freemantle to Adelaide Kruk and Bray, another A.B, took me aside and told me to be aft by the after wheelhouse as soon as it started to get dark and to wear my navy blouse.

When I got there, they were doing the usual exercise walking up and down the starboard side on the afterdeck where they were screened from view of anyone else on the ship. I was told to lay down and they grabbed me by the ankles and lowered me over the side, directly above the Lazavet porthole. Then they passed me a lever and told me to break the board of the box side and then pass the apples up to Bray. It was no problem to break the flimsy box open, I think one apple fell into the sea, as did the lever but I managed to pass the whole lot up to Bray, then turn and pull the box out through the porthole and drop it into the sea. Then of course, the porthole cover fell into place, and as luck would have it, so did the dog which clamped it tight. The apples were split amongst the seaman and stokers.

We never heard how the steward accounted for them, they were captains perks and he probably never heard of their loss, also during this run, Kruk discovered that No 1 hold had, on the second deck down, cases of nestles chocolates, and café au lait, besides malted milk etc. when the holds had been opened in Freemantle No 1 hold on the first deck down had been loaded with laurels and 44 gal drums of oil, these had been unloaded at Freemantle and we had to clear the deck of dunnage, that is the timber used to keep the drum from knocking against each other and causing sparks which might cause a fire, so they have to be packed and shored with baulks and pieces of timber so they can't move.

Now the deck was empty and there was a door leading from this deck to just near the bosuns cabin. Kruk had found a way to open this door, he and the ordinary seaman went in one dogwatch, lifted the tarpaulin which covered the hatch, broke open a case which contained chocolate, removed it, and divided it up amongst us, but somehow the mate, during his inspection got suspicious and opened the hatch and of course saw the broken case. He came up on deck and had all hands-on deck while he and the bosun conducted a search of the crew's quarters. I was very frightened because I had about 12 bars of chocolate under my mattress, where Kruk had put them, but peculiarly nothing was found, and it was blamed on the stevedores, but whenever I looked under my mattress there would be a bar of chocolate. I never saw it put there and never knew where it came from.

It was after leaving Freemantle that the bosun made what I consider to be another attempt to get rid of me. We were emptying dunnage from No 3 hold, and I was stationed on the small auxiliary hatch near the alleyway under the bridge superstructure and adjacent to the ships side. Vesey was on the other small hatch on the starboard side, as per sketch.

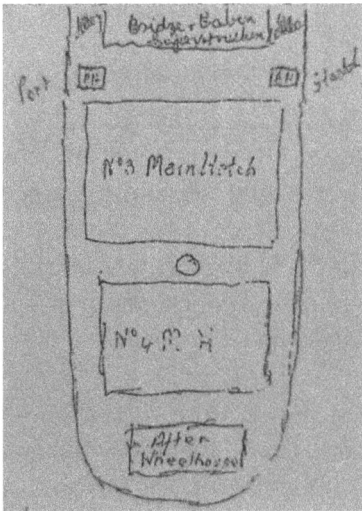

These hatches were about 4 ft 6 in square and I was just bending forward to take some timber to throw over the side when the bosun ran out from the alleyway and charged right into me, luckily, I had one hand on the coaming and involuntarily vaulted clean over the hatch, I stumbled and when I turned round, he told me to watch what I was doing. When I told Kruk, I said that I couldn't believe a man could be so vicious, but he was very grave, shook his head and said that one man had gone overboard accidently on purpose and that the sea kept its own secrets.

Well, we arrived in Melbourne and unloaded some more cargo including some iron. At that time no one had any inkling of the mineral wealth of this country and so imports played a major part in its development.

This time No 2 hold was cleaned right out, and we had to sweep and clean the hold right out. Then it was steam cleaned and the ship's engineers had the job of fastening a series of big pipes all around the ship's sides in the hold. This was to be one of the refrigerated holds to take carcasses of beef at Sydney. Mutton was to be loaded in New Zealand.

It was while steaming from Adelaide to Melbourne that I had a remarkable mental or spiritual experience. I remember it was Sunday, and a calm bright day with a nice light breeze, and it was my usual habit on Sunday mornings to go right up into the bow of the ship, lie on my tummy and stare down at the water breaking from the stem, also I could see the dolphins, effortlessly keeping just ahead of the stern. This morning, the day being perfect, I lay down as usual, watching the water being pushed aside by the ship's stern, when suddenly I was no longer just a boy lying there but a part of everything. I was still me, but also everything else, the water, the clouds, the ship, the wind. I can't really describe it; it was marvelous, and I've never had such an experience since. Although I tried to recapture it time and time again.

Eventually we arrived in Sydney and tied up at the Woolloomooloo, it was while we were hoisting the derricks from their crutches that the bosun and I clashed for the last time. Vesey was bending down attempting to turn the hoisting wire round the shackle wheels at the base of the mast, the bosun told me to give him a hand and as I bent down to do so, he struck me a sharp blow on the back of my neck. I'm not clear now as to just what happened then, as I literally saw red and went completely berserk. I recovered my senses with Kurk and Bray holding me in a tight grip and the mate telling me that I would be reported to the captain.

Apparently, I tried to put the bosun over the side and would have done so if I had not been stopped by Kruk and Bray. I didn't know until then how powerful one could be when they really let go. I was marched up to the captain and he asked me why I tried to drown the bosun, I said that he struck me first and I just lost my temper and, in any case, the bosun had tried to get rid of me and I intended on going to the shipping master and lodging a complaint. The captain told me that if I didn't behave myself that he would have to log me and that wouldn't help me with the navy.

The mate escorted me back to the deck and on the way quietly informed me that if I went to the shipping master there'd be an accident on the way home and I wouldn't see England again. I think that he was only trying to frighten me as otherwise, he'd always shown me a friendly manner. The next afternoon, I drew 5/- from the captain and went ashore by myself, I wandered up to the missions to seaman in George Street North. I was wearing my navy cap with T.S Arethusa on the band, navy jersey, and serge trousers.

CHAPTER FIVE: AUSTRALIAN IMPERIAL FORCES

I was sitting reading a magazine when I felt a tap on the shoulder, looking up I saw a trooper of the Light Horse and he said, "Hello Arethusa, how's the old barge doing?", I asked him who he was, and he said "come for a walk, I'm Warspite" naming the training ship for homeless and delinquent boys, which had been moored ahead of the Arethusa. So, we went for a walk, and he told me a tale of leaving Warspite, taking a ship to Canada and joining the mounted police there, while there he was sent out to arrest a man, couldn't catch up with him and ended up taking a ship to Australia and there joining the White Horse.

How much was the truth or not was anyone's guess, but he was friendly, and we had a similar training background. His name was Fred and when I had told him my tale, he said, "don't go back to the ship, come and join up". When I protested, I was too young he said, "you weren't too young for the navy, and you can say you're 19 1/4". I agreed and we went out to the showground, which was also the recruiting center, having been taken over by the army. To the sergeant at the table in the office Fred said, "this is my cousin, and he wants to join up and come away with me". The sergeant didn't even look up, but said "how old are you?", "19 ¼ Sergeant". He grabbed a form, did some writing, "name", "Honey, Sarge", "address", "c/o peoples palace", "ok, sign here, what unit do you want?", "Light Horse Sergeant." "Good, you're in the infantry, report to the corporal at the Poultry Pavilion". So, I'd joined the Australian Imperial Forces as a private on Thursday 19-1-1917.

On reporting to the corporal, he took my name and said go home and finish all your business if any and report back here at 7:30am tomorrow Friday 20th. So, we left, took a train into town, and went and sat in the domain right opposite where we could see the Port Campbell moored. Sitting on a bench talking who should come along but some of the crew, Prendergast young Vesey, the O.D. the Dane, the Finn, -I've forgotten their names, even if I could pronounce them- Prendergast said, "where have you been, the mates ropeable about you and you'll get hell when you get back aboard". Fred chipped in then and said, "hold your horse's mate, he's my cousin and I'll see him aboard before you sail". Prendergast said, "he'd better come with us, we are sailing first thing tomorrow". All Fred said was he'll be there, on your way, he's with me for the present I'm sailing tomorrow to France, and I might never see him again".

So, they went their way and Fred, and I booked rooms at the people's palace run by the salvation army. Bed and breakfast for 1/6d and a very good breakfast too. Porridge, bacon and eggs or steak and eggs, lashings of both brown and white bread, a whole pot of tea, great slabs of butter on the tables together with a big jar of celery and radishes and a bottle each of Worchester and tomato sauces. Food was plentiful and cheap, you could buy 21 tickets for 21 shilling, and this entitled you to three meals a day for 7 days and what meals, as much as any hungry man or boy could handle. Fruit also was plentiful and very cheap, some restaurants even had dishes of fruit on the tables, and you helped yourself, no extra charge and with the exception of breakfast meals were always three courses.

Incidentally, Fred spoke more truly than he knew when he told Prendergast that he was sailing to France on the Friday at 8am and he went aboard the transport that Friday night, but not to France but to Egypt.

I duly reported to the showground at 7:30am on the Friday, wondering all the while if I should be hauled back to the ship by police, but what happened was that nothing was done until she returned from

Sydney to New Zealand to top off her cargo and then I believe my things were sent ashore to the Shipping Master. I think that that was the end of the matter and of course no word got back to England that I had left the ship and joined the army.

On that Friday my clothes were taken and I was issued blue dungarees 2 piece, 1 slouch hat, 1 pair army boots, 2 pairs woolen socks, 2 grey flannel singlets, 1 cap (peaked), 2 "Australia" shoulder badges, 2 rising sun lapel badges, 1 large rising sun hat badge, 2 woolen singlets, 2 woolen long johns, 2 khaki shirts, 1 cut throat razor, 1 shaving brush, 1 comb, 1 hairbrush, 1 clothes brush, 1 toothbrush, 1 tin toothpaste, teeth for the cleaning of, 1 jacket army khaki but no trousers.

I was then told I could have weekend leave if I wanted it but to be sure and be back by 7:30am as we would then be sent to camp, in the meanwhile I would have to wear the dungarees with the khaki jacket. So, on Saturday I took the tram into the town and just wandered round and saw the sights. I'd been paid 10/- for Friday and Saturday and I concluded that I joined a ragtime army. After navy discipline everything was so casual and seemingly haphazard. In fact, the boys had a jingle sung to the tune "from Greenland's Joy Mountains to India's Coral Strand" and it went like this:

We are the ragtime army, the Aussie Infantry

We cannot shoot, we don't salute

What bloody good are we

And when we get to Berlin the kaiser he will say

"Hoch, Hoch! Mein Gott, what a bloody rotten lot"

To earn two bob a day

But make no mistake, they were real men.

I did not go to the Peoples Palace again, but I went
back to the showground each night, so I was already
there when Reveille sounded on the Monday
morning.

We were paraded at 8am on that Monday and taken
to the QM stores and issued with our trousers and
colour patches, rifles bayonet, entrenching tool,
pack and hover blankets, another jacket, and the
necessary leather equipment- this leather was
changed on arrival in England to the regulation
wellbeing equipment. Then a kitbag and housewife
were added, this had needles and thread already in –
one pair of puttes, one more pair of woolen socks.
After being checked to make sure we, all had a full

kit, we were sent back to the poultry shed and told to pack all our gear in the kitbags and pack.

We were shown how to roll our overcoats which were to be carried over the pack, then we marched to the necropolis section of central station, presumably as a security measure so that people wouldn't know where we were going. There we joined the train, and we were taken to Liverpool Army Camp. We were kept at the camp for about a fortnight. We arrived in Liverpool on the 22nd of January 1917. We did a bit of squad drill and guard duty but mostly just hung around, waiting for meals, and shooting off to Sydney.

I stayed in the camp and on February the 5th, men were selected to go as an advanced party to the Pyrmont wharf to prepare the "Wiltshire" and get her ready to take the troops. Some of the advance parties were married men and they protested that they wouldn't be able to say farewell to wives and children, so volunteers were called to take their place, and of course, I was one.

That night we were taken by train and tram to the wharf and set to work to load hammocks, equipment, kitbags, etc. and familiarize ourselves with the layout of the ship. The Wiltshire was a large and I think twin screw freighter of the "Shire" line and was fitted out as a troop ship. Colonel Dobbie was in charge and prior to volunteering, we had been promised a few hours leave prior to leaving, but Dobbie later reneged on this, and we were not even allowed on the wharf, but kept aboard the ship by police.

We worked hard all day on the 6th, getting things loaded and putting up directional notices. Decks were numbered as were the five holes, for example, The first deck down was A deck, the next one down B, right through the ship. No1 hold was A1 and B1. No2 was A2 and B2 and so on. Then next morning very early, the troops came aboard, it was barely light and soon after we cast off with the men lining the rails shouting goodbyes and waving to the crowds on the wharf. So much for security and secrecy.

As we left the harbour, we were told to come and collect our pay on the last day on 5/- a day. From the moment of embarking on February 7th we were to receive an extra 1/- a day as deferred pay. I was the first of our unit to get paid, as all the rest were waving goodbyes to friends and relatives who came along in ferries and launches to see us off.

We had two lieutenants, Lt. Harries and Davis, and it was their job to pay us. Mr. Harries asked me how long I had been in Australia and when I told him "A fortnight" they both thought that it was funny. We left Sydney on our own and a lot of the men were seasick at first. We had physical jerks in the mornings and in the evenings, the men just sat around and played cards, crown, and anchor or two-up. I made friends with another Englishman who I only knew as Gordon and an Australian who had been an American marine, Legen, they were both quite God-fearing men and when jokingly telling Legen that I didn't believe in God, he was very upset, until I assured him that it was far from the case. Legen was an artist at handling a rifle, he could do anything with it except make it talk. Since seeing the American magazines at the Edinburgh Tattoo, he was a corporal with us and one of the first to get killed in France.

Another good friend, who is still with us at the time that I write this, was Ben Ash, a superb shot, he taught me to shoot when we arrived in England; but I'm getting ahead of myself. On the voyage to Freemantle, we picked up a couple of other ships, and at Freemantle we were marshalled into a convoy of 6 ships, if my memory serves me right, we were marshalled in two lines.

The port ships were Asterley, followed by Wiltshire, followed by Ayrshire. The starboard ships were Nestor, followed by? forgotten, then Ajana.

Ajana was the slowest in the convoy and we usually lost sight of her during the day as we would all belt along then slow down at night for her to catch up. The trouble was that she was an old ship, and she made a lot of smoke, we didn't know it at the time but a German raider was about and Ajana's smoke would have been visible for miles, so we left her during the day and let her catch up at night.

The voyage as far as Durban was fairly uneventful, but at Durban we put into coal and as soon as we came in sight of land, we could see a figure on the headland waving to us, Miss Campbell! She met every troop ship that called in at Durban and came to them with baskets of fruit for the troops. All the boys knew about her and after the war the R.S.L invited her as a guest to Australia, she came, and we tried to show her how we had appreciated the way she welcomed the Aussie and New Zealand troops.

When we left Durban, (we had been taken ashore only once for a route march), we were shepherd by a light cruiser H.M.S Swiftshore, all the way to Capetown and here we were allowed shore to leave for 24 hours, all to be back aboard by 11pm.

I with five others and Corporal Leger were selected for picquet duty ashore, our job was to parade around the outskirts of the black's quarters and prevent any of the troops from going in there as there was supposed to be venereal disease among the blacks. As the troops didn't get ashore until lunch time, we were sent ashore ahead and reported to the police station. We were issued with batons and armlets, although we had our side arms (bayonets). It was a very uninspiring job, we marched around the streets surrounding the black's quarters and turned back any soldier who tried to go in there. Needless to say, some got through and if we caught them on the way back, they were arrested and marched to the police station, where they were locked in a cell.

We were relieved at 4pm by another squad and went back to the ship for tea, then back at 8pm until 11pm, where we were supposed to round up any stragglers and send them back aboard. At 10:30 pm things had become very quiet, no troops about at all, so we stood as a squad just around the corner from the police station, waiting for 11 pm, as it happened there was a fruit shop open just in front of us and after a while the proprietor came out and told us how proud he was to see us there, on our way to fight for his and our countries. He told us that he had a son fighting with the S.A Forces in East Africa and invited us to help ourselves to whatever fruit we liked.

Most of us thought that an orange or two would be useful but the proprietor wouldn't have it, he brought out 7 large, and I mean large, brown paper bags and insisted that we fill them. As we were supposed to be still on duty Leger told two men to collect the fruit, the rest of us marched off for a final look around the area. Then when we returned the two men left behind had filled the bags with apples, pears, bananas, oranges, and a great bunch of grapes on top. This was a problem at first as we couldn't take them to the police station, so we left one man to guard the bags and then went and signed off at the station, then collected our mate and the bags and back to the ship. There was so much fruit that we divided it amongst the men on our mess deck and it was very much appreciated.

The next day, our men were not allowed ashore, except those who had been on picquet duty, so Leger, Gordon and I went back to the fruit shop and presented the proprietor with a letter of thanks and appreciation from the boys of the 19th Reinforcements to the 17th Battalion and he said he would frame it and put it in his shop.

That night we in the Wiltshire were marched ashore to attend an invitation concert arranged by the mayor of Cape Town and put on by the school children of the school. We were a bit apprehensive as we thought that a school children's concert would be a rather boring affair, but surprisingly, it turned out to be a very enjoyable evening. Apart from our boys, all Cape Town who was anybody was there. It was held in the town hall and though now I don't remember all the details, the singing was very good. All I now remember was one extraordinary, beautiful girl, about 14, who sang "Grow Grow Grow Little Mushroom Grow". I fell for her very hard, of course I never saw her again, but I've never forgotten her or the song.

CHAPTER SIX: RETURN TO ENGLAND

I forgot how long we stayed in Cape Town, but we eventually left for the long trip North to England, but this time we had I think eight ships in the convoy and the bounty class cruiser H.M.S Kent. The Kent escorted us as far as Sierra Leone, which we saw in the distance and then we were on our own.

After some days of slow traveling but beautiful weather, approaching nightfall, we saw away on the horizon a faint light and at 2 am the next morning we were roused out of our hammocks and told to get fully dressed, stow our gear in our kitbags and report on deck by 2:30 am. At that time, we were mustered on deck and issued with dry rations for 24 hours also with 500 rounds of ball ammunition. We were told that the idea was to get munitions to England. Typical high brass thinking. I hate to think what would have happened had we been torpedoed, as was one other ship in the convoy. We were belting along at full speed, each ship for itself. A fleet of destroyers had come out during the night and each ship was escorted by one.

I couldn't see the other ships except the Asterley, belting along ahead of us, but we saw the flash and heard the tremendous explosion of the ship that was torpedoed. she must have been carrying ammunition and if so, the Germans were either well informed or else just lucky, for I doubt there were any survivors.

We were lucky and at about 6 am we docked at Falmouth. Had we been sunk, none of us could have survived as with all our gear and the 500 rounds we would have sunk like stones. Why the ammunition couldn't have remained in the boxes and been unlocked with the other stuff, I'll never know, unless they wanted it delivered quickly to the camps for use on the riffle ranges in England.

But to get back to Falmouth, it was the beginning of April, if I remember correctly and towards the end of one of the worst winters in memory. There was snow everywhere and it was bitterly cold and there we stood on the guard side with all our gear and rifles for two solid hours. We hadn't had anything to eat since tea the night before and our iron rations consisted of ships biscuits and 1 tin of bully beef between 4 men and they were small tins.

Eventually our train arrived, and we crowded aboard and set out for the trip to Salisbury Plain. Twice we were shunted onto a siding to let other troop trains pass going the other way. On these occasions the boys would pile out and indulge in snow fights. Many had never seen snow before and were like big kids.

Sometime during the morning, we arrived at Plymouth and here we stopped for a while, while the Lady Mayoress and a lot of helpers supplied us with sandwiches, tea and cake, which was most welcome and appreciated. The only problem being that we didn't stay long enough to have more than a few bites at the sandwiches and sip at the tea before we were off again and many of us missed out altogether. All that day we stopped, moved, and shunted about until we didn't know which way we were going, and it was bitterly cold. We had eaten our rations earlier and we had got nothing more after the Plymouth stop. It was 1 am the next morning when we eventually arrived at Amesbury station where we were unloaded and formed up in marching order and set off for Rollestone camp. A guide had met us at the station, and he led the way, the trouble was it was pitch dark and 2 ft of snow covered the ground and somehow, he got off the road. We were lost and we could only march on, stumbling into snow filled trenches and staggering into bits of barbed wire. We'd obviously become caught up in one of the training areas, but eventually we saw a light ahead which proved to be the orderly room of an artillery unit at Larkhill. Here we were put on the right track and at 3 am we arrived at Rollestone camp, tired, dispirited, ready for a good sleep and food.

But the Tommy Sgt Major was waiting for us and first we had to hand over our 2 new aussie blankets and be issued with two thin threadbare ones that you could shoot peas through. The S.M told us that our good blankets were wanted for the boys in France, but I doubt they ever saw France; (there were rackets in the first world war even as in the second). We were next marshalled to the mess huts and were issued with a tin plate, cup, knife, fork and spoon. Then a dixie of what he called stew was brought in and each of us was given one ladle of brown watery fluid and two slices of dry bread.

Well, we knew that there was rationing in England and that there was a scarcity of commodities, but our ship had -apart from the troops- been packed as tight as she could hold with tin fruit, Tassie apples, jam, butter, New Zealand mutton, Aussie beef, flour etc. and more had been taken on in South Africa. I silently questioned where it all went, I never heard of the troops even seeing it after we had arrived in England. Moreover, the other ships were likewise loaded with food and ships were coming into England from all over the world and while the subs were certainly doing a lot of damage, it was nothing to what it became in the Second World War.

Nevertheless, although we'd had practically nothing to eat and only two hours sleep, we were roused out at 6 am the next morning for physical jerks, wearing only woolen singlets, trousers, boots and socks. Then came breakfast at 7 am. A dixie of porridge to each table, 2 slices of dry bread, 2 tins of plum and apple jam and a dixie of tea.

Muster at 8 am and medical inspection, then we handed over our leather equipment which was replaced with webbing. Then we were split into platoons, one platoon would do squad drill, another would do marching, another bayonet practice, another rifle drill. Our N.C.O's were all reduced to privates and our officers were sent off to do the O.T.C. There they would have to learn how to be an officer all over again and trained by N.C. O's who had earned their stripes on the battlefield.

Our new Sgt Major was a young man named Gilbert who had won his warrant on the battle ground in France. So, the training went on for three months and then we were told that we were entitled to four days disembarkation leave prior to being sent to France.

Collecting our leave passes, we were given a final talk exhorting us to behave ourselves while on leave and not get into trouble, as previously Australians had been playing up when on leave. Then my company, about 40 men marched off to make our way to Amesbury station, which was a few miles away from our camp at Rollestone. We marched in formation until we passed Larkhill camp, then we broke formation on reaching the main road.

Coming down the road behind us was a big war dept lorry, driven by two conscientious objectors. These were men conscripted into the army, who refused to fight, ostensibly on the grounds that their conscious wouldn't allow them to kill. So, they were put into noncombatant jobs like transport drivers.

This lorry was loaded with German prisoners being taken to work on the farms around the area, they were all big men, mostly from the Russian guards. Their guards were two tommy soldiers, old men, not fit enough for the firing line but put on guard duties and they were walking along about ¼ mile behind the truck and were armed with carbines.

Somebody amongst us shouted "Are we going to march while these bastard's ride! Anyone drive a truck?". Somebody could, so we bundled the prisoners out, we all got in the truck and drove off, leaving the two guards pounding along and shouting to us to stop. I was a bit scared and wondered what would happen to us, but my mates weren't worried and were laughing and singing.

We pulled up short of the station at Amesbury and all marched down from the road onto the platform which was crowded with men going on leave. The train was waiting at the station, and it was crowded but we squeezed our way in and got safely mixed up with the others.

The Tommy guards had got work through Larkhill guardroom and the R.T.O. A lieutenant was vainly trying to push through the crowd to find the culprits but the crowded mass on the platform had got the word and of course, they did their best to hinder him, in fact, he was unable to move more than a foot at a time. He shouted at the engine driver to hold the train, but he took no notice and just blew his whistle and away we went.

It was getting dark by the time we got to London, as we had stopped a few times along the way; we were supposed to report to the Australian H.Q in Horseferry Road but the train stopped at Vauxhill station for some reason. The station was in darkness, but I got out as this was close to home and when I told my mates what I was doing, they decided to get out too. We had to climb over the lattice work gates to get out of the platform, but that was no problem, and I was soon on my way after explaining to my mates where we were and how they could get to the strand and Westminster. Then I marched down Kennington Road until I came to Prince's Road and so towards the house. About 50 yards from the house, I passed a policeman on his beat. I wished him a good night as I passed, and he stopped and watched me.

I knocked at the door and mum put her head out of the upstairs window "who's that"? "me" I said, "come down and let me in". it was very dark, the streetlamps were hooded and gave very little light, and the policeman started to walk towards me, "you are not coming in here", mum said "go away". The policeman quickened his pace, I said "don't be silly, it's only me, come down and let me in". With a curious note in her voice, mum said "who is it"? "me" I said, "not Bob" said mum "of course" said I, and the next minute she was down the stairs and the door flew open and she had her arms around me.

The policeman who we knew as "Darky", asked if everything was alright. Mum said, "it's only Bob" as if it was the most natural thing in the world for a stranger in Australian uniform to come along and demand to be let in, of course, she wanted to stay up and hear all that I had been doing, but I insisted on her going to bed and we could talk in the morning. When you come to look at it, I suppose it is a bit strange to have a son go away as a sailor, receive word that he had been presumed drowned at sea, then no word for 8 months and then have him turn up in the uniform of a strange army, but she took it quite calmly, as she said, she never did believe that I drowned.

What happened was that when I did not turn up, the ship sailed and I presumed that when she returned to Sydney, my things, if not already disposed of were sent to the Shipping Master. Anyway, the Port Campbell was torpedoed and sunk on the way home, with all hands going down but I have a strong feeling that Kruuk also left the ship, as many years later at Redcliff in Victoria, I saw a man get aboard a train there and if it wasn't Kruuk then it was a remarkable double.

Well, I had my four days leave and returned to Rollestone camp, preparing myself for the ordeal of entraining for France and fighting Germans but the good Lord had other ideas for me, for which I am now very thankful, for when we returned to camp we were told that we had to get further training and some of our men were drafted into other units but inevitably, the day came and we were mustered on the parade ground with all our gear. Then the St Major shouted for all men under the age of 19 years to take two places forward.

Three or four stepped out but I stood fast although Leger on one side of me and Doyle on the other urged me to step out. I was scared of course but since I started with them, I wanted to stay and finish with them. Then Major Hale, who had been scanning the ranks, came along and stood in front of me, "how old are you, honey"? "19 ¼, Sir" I replied, "you were 19 ¼ when you joined up! Don't you grow any older" "yes, Sir" I replied, "alright" said the Major "what was the date of your birth"? I did some very quick mental arithmetic and came up with the 22 September 1898; he said, "you had to stop and think about that one" I said, "yes Sir, I wasn't expecting it", "I'll say you weren't, carry on" he said and went.

We were dismissed back to the huts to get a meal and then Sgt Major Gilbert mustered the company between the huts, ready to march down to the train which had pulled right into the camp on the supply line. I was shivering partly from excitement and partly from fright at the thought of going to France and into the firing line. I think we were all a bit scared; things weren't going to well in France and we had seen the hospital trains loaded with wounded and maimed men.

I had also visited the St Thomas's Hospital where dad oversaw the army medical Corp doing the cooking and I had seen the mutilated and battered men returned from France. I was under no illusions about the so-called glory of fighting for your King and country. The only thing I was scared about was whether I would be able to stand up to it or whether I would get so scared that I'd panic and run away, and I knew that I wasn't the only one who felt that. It wasn't so much the thought of dying as of being shattered and maimed and no one knows just how he will behave until that moment of truth, but to go on, as the man mustered, Gilbert called out "Private Honey report to the orderly room".

So, I went along to the orderly room and to the adjutant Captain Cook, he asked me to sit down and then said, "how old are you really Honey", "19 ¼ Sir", "you're sure of that?" "Yes sir", "you know Honey, fighting in France isn't a picnic, it's just plain bloody murder, there isn't any adventure or glory in it and if you have any ideas about that get rid of them now. I don't believe you are 19 by a long way and do you know what will happen to you if you get over there and they find you are under age" I said "No Sir" "well" he said, "they will charge you with attempting to murder his Majesty's enemies without the permission of the Allied Forces and you will get 90 days in the glasshouse, so, what we are going to do, is to transfer you to the army medical corps, where you will be a non-combatant, we just don't believe you".

I should have had a feeling of relief but instead I only felt angry, I thought he was trying to scare me with the talk of murdering his Majesty's enemies and I protested that I wanted to stay with my mates but he cut me short, took my pay book and told me I was to draw dry rations and march out to Parkhouse Camp near Tidworth together with the lads who had stepped out being under 19. When I got my paybook back my age was altered to 17 and his initials were beside it G.B.

So, my mates marched down the train and Frances and I and a couple of others marched out for Parkhouse.

When we got to Parkhouse, I was amazed at the number of lads there that were under 19, we practically made up a company, but of course, there were a large number of grown men as well. Life was fairly easy there, the food wasn't too bad, although never enough. It was summer and the weather was beautiful, they didn't trouble us younger folk very much. We of course had to learn stretcher drill, how to render first aid and go through the gas hut with and without masks. our officers were doctors and were mostly continuously changing as they had a short period of training battalions for a few weeks before going to France.

We had one permanent officer D' Bellamy who was a nice old fellow, too old for France and no soldier. He used to take us for route marches, or, when as sometimes happened, we had too many men in the depot to handle, we would be divided into two lots. A couple of footballs would be thrown in between and there would be wild scrimmages, as everyone would barge in and get at the balls to try and kick a goal. No one cared about sides and the result was that there were a few injured and Major Seymour, who was the Camp Commander, had them stopped.

The Parkhouse camp was also a staging camp, and men who had been wounded and recovered were sort there for re-drafting and so sometimes there would be as many as 300.

On one of our slack days, a couple of mates and I walked over to Tidworth and got ourselves tattooed (a stupid thing to do). I was to have the R.M. Corp insignia of a snake with staff on my right arm in three colours, red, blue, and black. This meant going over the tattoo three times. First, he drew the snake on the arm, then will the electric needle, he went over the lines in black, then with red, then blue. This was fairly painful, and I began to feel a bit sick. I said that I would leave the staff to be done next time, paid him 2/6 and left. I never did go back to get the staff done, first because he'd put the snake upside down, and secondly because I was transferred to Battalion detail where I would take the place of a man who would go to France.

We went back to camp and the Sgt Major called me and another lad into the orderly room, handed us our files and a note to the doctor of the unit we were to go to and sent us off.

I was told to go to Larkhill and the other chao to Rollestone, so away we marched. When we were about halfway, I asked the other chap if he knew anyone at Rollestone. He said no that he had originally come from Larkhill, so I suggested we swap notes, he'd go to Larkhill and I to Rollestone. He demurred at first, saying that we'd get into trouble, but I pointed out that the transfer forms were exactly the same, both addressed to the C.O of the two camps, didn't mention the destination, simply said that Private so's and so's file was sent as a medical orderly to be under the command of the medical officer of the Battalion. So, we swapped the notes, mine having been addressed to the C.O. of Larkhill and his to the C.O. of Rollestone. So, I attached his note to my file, and he attached mine to his, everyone was happy, and we got away with it. I don't think it made any difference and I doubt if anyone noticed, probably if I had asked Sgt Major to send me to Rollestone, he would have told me to please myself. The main thing was that somebody turned up to replace the man sent to France. That was what they used us for, to replace able bodied men who were capable of fighting.

There was not a great deal to do at the Rollestone camp. I had to get the room ready for sick parade, obtain from the Sgt Major the men for disposal of garbage cans, inspect the latrines, washhouses, and grease traps to see they were kept clean. We had a Serjeant who had been a health inspector, and this was his job, but he would deputize me for hat while he inspected the meat, cookhouse, and perishable foodstuffs but when he went on leave, I had to do the lot. I also had to oversee the treatment of sick men and the preparation of the sulfur baths for men who had scabies, - an infectious skin disease caused by a minute parasite. This meant blocking the outlets of the showers and filling the floor of each shower cubicle with sulfur solution. Each patient had to sit in this and then rub himself all over with a brush dipped in the solution, had to do his back. They had three days out of five for this and the last two days they were treated with carbolassers ointment which was simply a mixture of Vaseline with a few drops of carbolic acid and some boracic powder worked in with a spatula. This invariably affected a cure then the man would be inspected by the Dr pronounced cured and sent back to duty. However, I had one man who was reportedly sent back, I asked the doctor about it, and he said that he was an obstinate case. This made me suspicious, and I pointed out to the Dr that this man was the only one in his hut who had scabies and why weren't the other men getting the disease which appears as an itchy rash between the fingers, toes and on the body. I also pointed out that he only had the rash on his back and chest not on fingers and toes.

The doctor looked thoughtful and then said, "bring him up to the empty hut, and keep him under observation". So, I brought him and his gear to the isolation hut which was empty. The next morning, as soon as Reveille went, I went to the hut and quietly opened the door and found him batting himself over the shoulder with a scrubbing brush which brought out red spots which at a glance looked scabious. He was paraded before the doctor who closely examined him and pronounced him malingering. He was up before the Colonel Nossie and sentenced to seven days and to be sent to France, however, from having had so many Sulphur baths he developed a very bad allergy rash and had to go to hospital.

One of the things that always puzzled us, was, that although we were strictly rationed two slices of bread per man for breakfast and tea, one slice for dinner at midday. Breakfast usually consisted of porridge in winter, perhaps a chop of piece of meat, one tin of jam amongst six men, dinner usually stew, or so-called stew followed by a pudding made mostly from scraps of crusts and crumbs from God knows where with perhaps a tin of treacle. Tea was two slices of bread and the usual plum and apple jam. The orderly officer would come around with the S.M. and ask any complaints, if someone did complain he was told that there was a war on, and the food was kept so that the men in the trenches could be fed.

This worked for a while and the men didn't complain, but when we had men who has been in the trenches among us there were some tough scenes, resulting in the rations being slightly improved until they came up with the cry that food was scarce because of the LL. Boats. Perhaps it was but why could we go down to the canteen, the YMCA and the Salvation Army and buy sausages and mash for 1/6. It was true the YMCA and the Sally's only had limited supplies and God knows how they got them, but the canteen run by the N.A.A.F.I, who were responsible for supplies, never seemed to run short and there was the black market, where if you had the right connections, you could get anything you wanted. Not that I ever got anything and never tried, but I have often wondered, how close a scrutiny, some of the new wealthy would have stood into the sources of their wealth. Thousands fought and starved so that they could live in comfort and wealth.

Well, to get on with the job, reading back, I see that I have forgotten to mention that when I arrived at Rollestone from Parkhurst, I found out within a day or so that the Dr there at the time was a drug addict. I reported to the Sgt Major and the next day that Dr was gone, most likely straight to France. I didn't like reporting this, but I had to restrict myself since a very strict account was kept of drug supplies and as I found that we were over the allowed amount, I might have been blamed. However, a Dr Railton arrived the next day, but he was only with us for a few days, then he went off to France.

Then Dr. Nowland arrived and a few days later the whole camp was transferred to FOVANT which was a camp just outside the quite little village of that name. Here the medical staff was enlarged by the addition of a chemist, who had been one of my reinforcements, and his name was Priscoll, more of him later. A corporal Hansen of the A.A.M.C was in charge under the doctor and his mate Jack Stafford of the same A.A.M.C was in charge of venereal cases, these two men had been wounded at Gallipoli, and again in France, they had been together right from the start. Norm Hansen's was a brewer in W.A while Jack Stafford was an American marine engineer, who had jumped ship to join the A.I.F.

So, I became a spare part, my job was offsider to Bill, who was our health inspector, which was his job in civil life also. I took charge of scabies and the infectious diseases hut, and I had to attend the first parade every morning to ask the Sgt Major to tell off six men for latrine and washhouse fatigues. I had to see that they did the job properly and in time for the colonel's and doctors' inspection. This was quite a circus in a way. First the colonel with the doctor, then Bill and me, it was a blasted nuisance at first since I had to leave my own job of supervising and bathing the scabies unit to follow them all around the camp, luckily, it didn't last. The colonel, Norrie, had his wife come and live in the village, so he left it all to the doctor. Then the doctor went to live in the village to be close to the colonel, as his wife was pregnant. So, he left it to Bill, who was a Sergeant. Bill told me to take care of the latrine details, the inspection of rubbish bins and the cleaning of grease traps. So, I had to get six men for latrines and washhouses, two men for the disposal of garbage and rubbish bins. This all had to be done on the first early morning parade.

The men picked for the fatigue didn't mind as it got them off the early morning physical drill and route marches and so long as they had the work done by breakfast at 8 am and done properly, I didn't bother them, so I could go ahead and take the names of men who had asked to go on sick parade. This was held at 9 am. The doctor and Norm Hansen would sit behind a table in the medical hut, and I would muster the men in the waiting room. Norm would call each man in turn by name from the list I had made. I would march him in, the doc would ask him what was wrong, and if he thought him sick, would examine him and if he found anything wrong, would send him back to his hut, where he would later visit him and decide if he could be left in his hut and excused parade, or go to hospital. Norm would note the doc's decision against the name on my list and I would later have to take the list down to the Battalion H.Q, if there were what Brigade considered too many on the sick list they would set up a scream to Batt H.Q, who would promptly pass the buck to us, but if doc Nowlane took a man off duty, he stuck to it and refused to be bluffed. As we had a lot of men who returned wounded from France and were nearly all on the convalescent list, this took a fair bit of guts as Brigade was always trying to urge the doc to declare men fit for duty.

On the other hand, if a man tried to put it over and at first, many did, they got short shift. Doc had a piece of lead on a string hanging from his cabinet on the side of the table and when he had a malingerer before him, he prescribed a No.9 and without the man seeing it, he would set the lead swinging. Norm would see this and make a note against the man's name, and that man would find himself on the next draft for France.

Mostly it was just coughs and colds, a few venereal cases who were sent to Jack Stafford for first treatment, then if not cleared up within 14 days, sent to Bulford venerea hospital. Once they went there, their pay stopped until they were cured, or died. If they died then they were posted as died from self-inflicted wounds, but this was later stopped out of consideration for their families. The cured ones were sent straight back to France.

CHAPTER SEVEN: EVERY MAN TO FRANCE

Life went on then things became bad in France and every man who could stagger on two feet was hurriedly rounded up and sent to France, so we had a fairly easy time for a while. Bill was transferred and I had to do his work, then women, the W.A.A.C (The Women's Army Auxiliary Corps), as they later became known became the mess orderlies in the officers and Sgts messes. They also took over the work in the canteens, then things eased again. It was now 1918 and only Driscoll, Norm, Jack and myself were left, then it was decided that any A.A.M.C man who had not been trained in the treatment of V.D had to attend a 14 day course at Bulford. As Norm and Jack had already done the course, doc decided that Driscoll had to go, and he was told to draw rations for 24 hours and march off to Bulford on his own, but precariously enough, that night he became ill, and doc had to be sent, for doc was no fool and he became suspicious, but he couldn't take a risk, so decided that I would have to go. So, I collected my file and rations from Batt. H.Q and set off. I got to Bulford about 2 pm and reported it to a sergeant in the orderly room, he detailed me to the laundry section and the corporal there issued me with a pair of sterile gloves and told me to go to the Sgt in charge of the O.P hut. I was just putting my gloves on when a doctor and a Major came in and saw me, "what the hell are you doing here?" he roared, "sent from 5th T.B detail" I said, "get to hell back there, we won't have any babies here".

I was a bit mortified but old enough to get out of there and back to Fovant. Doc was not surprised, but decided that Driscoll had put it over, as he had recovered fairly quickly, so he put his name down for the next draft to France, but when a week later Driscoll was told to get his gear ready and move out the next morning, he had a heart attack that night. Doc was called and decided to send him to the hospital, he was pretty sure it had been brought on, but he couldn't prove it and couldn't take the risk, so he sent him to the hospital. Well! There is some point in being a chemist, the next we heard, Driscoll had been sent home and discharged.

Then came the time the Allies had been waiting for, every available man was pulled in, myself included. I was pulled out of the medical details and put in the bull ring, once again I wore my old colours. Black over green diamond, 17th Batt. And for four weeks we did Bayonet fighting squad drill, route marches and physical drill. Then H.Q sent for me, Sgt Freemantle came for me early in the morning and asked for my pay book. I accompanied him down to H.Q certain now that I would get to France, Brigade was on the phone, "was Honey 19?", "no sir, Captain Cook contacted his parents and found that he is only 18", "we are not concerned about that, did cook alter his paybook?", "yes sir, altered and initialed G.B", "damn! Send him back, we can't risk it".

Apparently if Captain Cook hadn't altered the paybook, they would have sent me to France. As it was, I was a bit upset as I had steeled myself to go and was quite willing although a bit scared, I asked Freemantle to rub the entry out, but he said it was in ink and he wouldn't anyway, that I was very lucky and only a bloody fool wanted to go into that bloodbath and to think myself lucky to get out of it and to hope it was over before I turned 19. Apparently, mum had written to the Colonel and pointed out that dad and two sons were in the British army and that I wouldn't be 19 until 1919.

So back I went to the camp, but this time as an infantry man and medical corps and they decided that I would be most useful on the Q.M staff. So, I was made acting Corporal without pay and as Bill had been sent away, I was given the job of inspecting meat, the cleaning of washhouses, latrines, garbage disposal from the Officers, Sergeants and men's cookhouses! But I jumped ahead a bit, before I was put on the Q. M's staff, I was sent as offsider to the Sgt's mess cook, one Louis, a big French Chinese half caste, but a superb cook. He had been second chef at the Hotel Cecil in London at one time, then the men started to disappear as the push advanced, so the rear echelons were moved over to France. The army medical section went first, then all the fit men, then N.C. G's and we were left with men and N.C. O's waiting a draft home.

CHAPTER EIGHT: THE ARMISTICE

I was given the job first as barman in the Sgt's mess and then came the armistice. As it happens, I was the first one to hear it as I had been down to H.Q to take the mess reports and I heard the orderly Sgt take the word over the phone. I immediately went to the canteen, where most of the men were, it being mess hour soon, but there was so much noise of talk that no one heard me. Lady Elizabeth who was serving as barmaid beckoned to me and I was hoisted onto the counter, that attracted their attention, and I was able to give the news. There was immediate spontaneous cheering, and I was told I would have to shout for the mob.

I never paid for any drinks, and I can only suppose Lady Elizabeth did. I don't know who she really was, some said she was Lord Derby's daughter, but I don't know if he had a daughter or not, but she did stop some of the boys trying to force me to drink a beer.

It was after the armistice that I was made a corporal and I always had a devil of a job to get men to do the fatigues as the men point blank refused to do anymore training and it was only after the colonel threatened to put any man on the blacklist, that anything was done at all. So, I usually got the six or eight men I needed, and the rest would be given games like cricket or football, and there was an attempt made to do some teaching of trades or schooling.

Although being put on the blacklist meant that they would be the last to be sent home, and the colonel insisted that it wasn't the end, only an armistice, and that war could start again, the men flatly refused to do anymore training. There were too many to punish and they were, anyway, so the colonel made the best of it but insisted they keep as fit as possible.

Then the order came for us to shift from Fovant to Hurdcott, about a mile or so up the road. When this order came out, the Q.M who was a captain, told me he had been ordered to France, then to Germany and asked me to go with him. He promised me Sergeant's rank and pay. He pointed out that there would be good opportunities for me, and I could perhaps remain in the permanent army. I wasn't interested and only wanted to get back to Australia, which shows how thoughtless one can be when young. Had I accepted the captain's offer, I would probably have made a career and perhaps lots of money, but I did think it was just possible that the navy might claim me as I had been signed on for 12 or 21 years.

However, we shifted to Hurdcott which had been set up to handle drafting and allotting of men for the voyage home. Here we were told that if we wanted to, we could have indefinite leave pay, even take a job, if so inclined. The idea being that it would make the job of returning the men back to Australia that much easier.

A good many took advantage of this offer, but I knocked it back, rather selfishly, I see now, thinking of only getting back to see the country and meet the girl I had been corresponding with, ever since the year before, that I opened a parcel she sent which was sent to a 'lonely soldier' and had been given to me by the Red Cross as I had told the authorities that I had no kin

At Hurdcott I was allotted to Colonel Doctor Moody, who was examining all men to be sent home. He had his son killed in France and I was sent to him because of my having been in the medical corps.

The idea was that the least fit men were to be placed in the boat list first, hence the exam. I had only been there a few days when he asked me if I would like to go home, naturally, I said I would and when he gave me the next list of names for men to go back, I found my name on the list. I wrote to mum and dad and told them that I would not be getting leave to see them, as my name was on the list to go back to - how selfish and thoughtless one can be. It never occurred to me that they would have liked me to go home and stay awhile, in fact, I didn't think they cared much about me at all – but dad and Alf actually came to see me at the camp and tried hard to get me to take my discharge in England, but I wouldn't even consider it and they went home disappointed.

After a day or so, my name went on the supplementary list for the S.S Demosthenes, this meant that I had to stand by incase some of the men on the main list failed to turn up. So that night at 8 pm the W.O (warrant officer) had the men whose names were on the list posted on the notice board mustered at the orderly room.

Those of us on the supplementary list had to muster separately, then came the process of calling the names of some 800 or so men, the list for another ship was called first, and then came our turn. As a man's name was called, he had to step forward and form part of the company for the Demosthenes. If he didn't come forward and hand over the pay book, his name was crossed off and a supplementary was called in his place. I was eighth on that list and I began to fear that I might miss this one, but just as the H.Q was nearing the end of his list, someone failed to appear, and my name was called. I stepped forward and handed over my paybook and my name was substituted for the missing man.

Eventually when the full company was mustered, we were told to collect all our gear and parade ready to march out, all we had to take was our clothes and kitbags and although it was nearly midnight, we were given rations and marched down to the train and then on to Plymouth. Here we boarded the ship and next morning we sailed, as far as I remember, we had fine weather all the way.

The officer in charge of the troops was Major Bruce, afterwards, a politician and later a Prime Minister and a right "b" he proved to be. He was all for making the troops do physical exercises and parades three times a day, he didn't seem to realize that the war was over, but the troops would have none of it, and very emphatically and descriptfully told him where to go. There wasn't any room on the ship anyhow, what spare space was available, was taken up with temporary washhouses and lavatories. Only the hatch covers and right up in the bows were clear and the bow was reserved for the crew.

There were two decks below the main deck, and these were divided into messrooms and sleeping quarters. Hammocks were provided and swung over the mess tables, my company was allotted to A1 deck, which was right up forward behind the crew's quarters. Beneath us was the A2 deck. And as you went further aft, you had B1 and B2 decks, then C1 and C2, D1 and D2. We were crammed to capacity and more, even the officers and nurses were cramped up to as many as four to a cabin. They were on the highest deck which was just below the bridge in the superstructure. The N.C. O's – sergeants and W.O had cabins beneath the officers, and they shared up to four cabins. The ships officers had their own cabins. The Demosthenes was not really a passenger ship but a cargo carrier with passenger accommodation, and our mess decks were the ships holds.

After leaving Plymouth we crossed Biscay and entered the Mediterranean passing Gibraltar and a marvelous sight it seemed with warships in the harbour.

Our first Port of call was Port Said with the statue of De Lesseps at the entrance of the canal. Here we anchored to wait until we could pass through the canal. We were quickly surrounded by the Gyppo's bumboatman who would try and sell you all sorts of stuff from filthy postcards to oranges, a basket of oranges was 2/-2 lb., beautiful oranges too. We passed through the canal and ran just before the bitter lake and were slewed across the channel. This was the fault of the pilot; he hadn't realized how heavily laden we were. Here the boys had a bit of fun as the Gyppo's tried to get the ship off and straightened out. A crew of boatmen rowed down the side to take a rope and then tried to pull the bows off the sand, but the boys thought it great fun to pelt them with potatoes that had gone bad. Eventually we got off and proceeded past Suez and out into the Red Sea! which isn't red but green. Here it became very hot and someone up on the upper deck, apparently from the sick bay, came out and jumped overboard, although we stopped, no sign of him appeared.

An 18th Batt ex-navy man and I were elected as mess deck sweeper and mess orderly respectively. It was my job to look after and prepare the meals for my table, of which there were five on our deck, two on each side and two in the center. I didn't cook the food, but I collected the dry rations for my deck and brought the meals from the galley. The other tables were each looked after by other chaps, but they only brought their meals from the galley and set up the tables. Bill was the mess deck sweeper, for these services, each man in the mess paid me 1/- per week. The ship's captain arranged competitions between the various decks with prizes for the cleanest and best kept mess areas. There was one prize for the best mess for the trip from Plymouth to Suez and one from Suez to Freemantle. We were lucky, for Bill and I teamed up and we used to scrub and holystone the tables, scrub the deck on our deck and we used to arrange the cutlery, pepper, salt, and vinegar containers in various patterns on the tables and since Bill and I took it on as a fulltime occupation and being navy trained, we won both times.

Eventually we arrived at Ceylon and anchored in Columbo harbour, here we were allowed ashore and after changing our money at the money changers on the quay, we set about exploring the city. It was very warm, and we walked along with our coats open, this showed our army issue grey flannel shirts, and before long we were followed by a group of urchins shouting at us and holding up cotton singlets. at first, we couldn't make out what they were after, but it turned out they were offering us two singlets in exchange for our flannels. Bill, being a bit of a character, said he wanted three singlets and they snapped him up. He took off his coat and flannel and promptly grabbed the three singlets, putting one on. I wouldn't be I it, but they appeared to be alright, and Bill didn't complain. Then we passed a barber shop, and the barber came out. He caught me by the arm "I give you free haircut, you go and tell your men come haircut with me", Bill said, "you give me free haircut too", "no! no! Only him" Bill said, "no good, you cut his hair, you cut mine". After a lot of argument, the barber agreed, and we both got a free haircut and well done too. The only thing was that Bill told all the diggers we met that this barber was giving free haircuts to the troops. I thought this wasn't playing the game, and I would tell them that Bill was joking but he thought it was a great joke.

We spent a fair time wandering around the bazaars and I wanted some silk to take as a present to the girl I had been writing to Rita but it was obvious that we would have been fools to bargain with these people. They revel in bargaining, and we couldn't understand them, so we went to the Y.M.C.A for a cup of tea and a bite to eat and the lady in charge said that she would take me to a silk merchant and get me a fair price, so I went with her, and I choose a beautiful light mauve coloured silk and got 4 yards for 10/-. We thanked the lady and departed back to the ship.

On the way we came across a Parsee on his knees in the middle of the pavement, apparently praying. And Bill without thinking booted him in the tail. We heard a shout behind us and there were two Sihk policemen with their long lathis shouting at us, so we ran, with them after us, we turned a corner and across a park of rubber trees and came on what we afterwards found was the governor's house. It was surrounded by a hedge and gardens, and we promptly ducked behind the hedge! One policeman appeared from the park and looked up and down and not seeing anyone, turned back and disappeared. After he had gone, we continued back to the ship, and I asked Bill what the hell he had to go and kick the bloke for. He replied that the temptation was too great to resist, and he did it more or less without thinking. The next morning the British police inspector came aboard with one of the Sihk policemen and made a complaint to the captain. He passed it over to Major Bruce and he asked the inspector if the Sihk could pick out the culprit. We were on deck when the Major, the Prospector, and the Sihk came along. Luckily, we were only wearing shorts and flannels at the time and although he looked hard at us, he didn't identify anyone, but Major Bruce stopped all further leave ashore.

Just after this event a Cingalese swam from a boat and climbed up the anchor chain to where we were in the bows and he offered me a ruby which he had in his mouth and wanted 10/- for it, of course the boys all gathered around. I asked if it was genuine, he asked me for two pennies, which he placed on the deck with the ruby in between, then asked me to stamp on it, which I did with the iron shod heel of my boot. It was about the size of a large pea, and although uncut, was a beautiful red. I expected it to be smashed to pieces but instead it cut through both pennies like a knife through butter, so it must have been genuine.

I would have given him the 10/- and so would any of the others, but the crowd attracted the attention of the inspector and policemen, and they came pushing through the crowd calling to us to hold the man. Instead, of course, we did our best to block his way and the man grabbed his ruby and the pennies and promptly dived overboard, and disappeared from sight, he could of course swim like a fish. The inspector said the man had smuggled the ruby from the mines and would go to goal when they caught him. He asked us if the man had rubies, but we said that he had only been touting for custom to take men ashore, of course he didn't believe us but couldn't do anything about it.

That night we sailed for Freemantle and on arrival there we disembarked the westrailion section, and were given a marvelous reception by the people, we were allowed ashore but were unable to spend anything. One of the warehouses on the quay had been fitted up as a canteen and here at any time of the day up till 11 pm at night, we could get free meals or snacks. It was run by the Woman's Voluntary Aid, and apparently paid for by the citizens, and cost us nothing. We had a run up to Perth on the steam train that ran along the streets, but the real setup was at Adelaide when we arrived there. Here again a warehouse had been set up as a huge canteen. Meals and foods of all kinds were available at all hours, moreover when we went into the town, as we did each day for the two days we were there. We couldn't spend any money, whatever we wanted when we went to pay for it the reply would be, "it's on the house". And this applied to the picture shows and theatres. There were also good concerts put on at night at the canteen. If I remember rightly, I think we also unloaded the Victorian contingent here, as I don't remember going to Melbourne, I believe we went straight to Sydney.

CHAPTER NINE: ARRIVING IN SYDNEY

I arrived in Sydney on March 6th, 1919, my 19th birthday, and we were met with instructions to berth at the quarantine station and be kept there a fortnight on account of the flu epidemic. The customs and health men were wearing gauze masks, but we had no sickness of any kind aboard, and we could see no reason why we should be kept aboard for a fortnight because of a flue in Sydney. So, we made quite a row, and in the end, we anchored off

Taronga Park. There we were unloaded onto ferries and taken to Woolloomooloo, where we found crowds of people cheering like mad and fleets of cars and taxis.

Another chap and I were bundled into an open car and sat on the back seat, as were all the other men, and we moved off in a long line up through the park to a hut where we were to be examined. I didn't know the other chap, but like me, he was nervous at all the crowds and excitement, and to make it worse, we proceeded to the park road which was lined by people held back by police, a woman rushed from the crowd crying "Jimmy, my Jimmy" and flung herself onto the chaps lap, and there she stayed despite the efforts of police to drag her back.

When we arrived at the hut in the park, a doctor examined us by feeling our necks and putting a stethoscope on our chests. The doctor asked me if I would like to go to Prince Henry Hospital and when I said "No", he said I was foolish, that I should go and have a fortnight's rest. I didn't realise until years later that the idea was to set up grounds for a pension.

However, when I left the doctor, I was directed to go through a tent and when I walked in who should be there but Captain Taylor, who had been our company commander. He handed me a five-pound note and said, "this is the gift of the people of Sydney, and I suppose Honey, you will be rushing to join up again when the bands start playing", "not me sir" I said, "I only want to get rid of this uniform".

There was one incident while crossing the Indian ocean that I forgot to mention. As I said, I was the mess orderly for my mess which was situated in the center of the mess deck, there were two messes on each side of the deck, thus right over on each ship side of the mess table, there was a porthole. These were heavy brass, and naturally had become green with verdigris owing to the salt spray.

The adjutant, who daily made an early round to see that everything was clean and shipshape for the major's 10 o'clock round, was a pompous type, who liked to throw his weight about, and although a captain, had not seen any active service but apparently had held down a desk job. On this particular morning, he couldn't find any fault with our deck, and for some reason he had us in his black book and looked around, trying to pick something to fault with. As the mess tables were scrubbed white, all utensils clean and shining and set out in attractive patterns, he suddenly noticed the portholes and walking over to the starboard mess tables curtly ordered both orderlies to get to work and polish their portholes. They refused, so he placed them all under arrest, then he told Bill to clean them. Bill told him to do them himself if he wanted them cleaned, then he told me I'd have to do them. I told him that the boys paid me to look after the two center tables, not to clean ruddy portholes. I said it was the crew's job to clean portholes, so Bill and I were also placed under arrest. The six of us were put in the clink. Which was a temporary structure on the starboard side of the upper deck, just clear of the ladder leading to our deck.

Of course, when mealtime came at 12 noon, there were no meals ready on our deck and when the boys found out what had happened, they demanded our release and the matter wiped out. When the adjutant came down, they threatened to throw him overboard, so he retreaded and Major Bruce came down and tried to reason with them, "we had" he said, "disobeyed a direct order from a superior officer, which was a crime according to KR&R". one of our sergeants was a lawyer in civil life and he promptly challenged Bruce, he asked him "did not the shipping company provide a crew to keep the ship clean?", Bruce agreed. Then said our sergeant "are not the portholes a part of the ship" Bruce agreed again, "then it must be the crew's job to clean the portholes and that being the adjutant gave an unreasonable order and the men were in order to refuse".

Bruce would not give in and there was a move to throw Bruce overboard and take over the ship. Then the ship's captain appeared and told Bruce that this was his ship and to release the men and stop this bloody nonsense, didn't he realise that the war was over, and the men were returning to civil life and could make things very unpleasant for Bruce and the adjutant. So, with a very bad grace, Bruce gave in, but was stupid enough to say that even if they did throw him overboard, he would have done his duty. At which the captain replied, "don't be such a pompous ass, and much good it would do you when you're floundering in the water".

But to get back to taws. After collecting my £5, I found an old friend who had been sent home earlier in the year, Alf, waiting for me and he took me home to meet his wife. Alf was over 60 – the reason he was sent home- but he'd married a much younger woman, and they wanted me to stay with them, but I wouldn't do this. I wanted to be free to get around and see something of the place, so I went and stayed at the Peoples Palace!

I had to report the next day, Friday, to return my overcoat, sign various forms and collect pay. Then I went along to Gowing Bros in George St and was measured for a suit, a good one of navy-blue twill and for shirts, underpants, tie, and hat. I also paid 1/- for my R.S.L badge which I joined that day. Unfortunately, no one told me that I was eligible for trade training at government expense, so I knew nothing about it.

I had to report to receive my final discharge the following Tuesday, but I had received another £5 from Captain Taylor on the Friday which he said was a gift from the people of N.S.W. So, from Friday until Tuesday I took tram rides to various places around Sydney and one round trip from

Sydney to Hawkesbury, -now Brooklyn-, by rail, then ferry to Narrabeen on Pittwater, then back by tram to central. I also booked myself on the S.S Burringbar for the trip to Woodburn on the North Coast to meet the girl I had been corresponding with during the war. As mentioned previously, she was a Miss Rila, and 4 years older than me, she had sent a parcel through the Red Cross, addressed to a dear lonely soldier, and as the army had given my name to the Red Cross as having no kin, I'd been given this parcel, and having written to the address inside, we had swapped photos and kept up correspondence.

So, on Tuesday I reported for my discharge, I received that and my badge and returned to Sydney to pick up my new suit. My uniform and army gear had all been left in my kitbag at the Missions to Seaman in George St North. I had made good friends with the padre there and he had got me to go around the ships anchored in the harbour on their launch, delivering papers and literature to them. At this time, the big American schooners were often to be seen here and in March 1919, there was one of the biggest. A five masted schooner, Helen B Stirling, anchored off Farmhouse Cove, and it was quite a thrill to see these ships at close quarters.

Now having fitted myself out, I went along to the shipping office to see how soon I could get onto the 'Burringbar', only to learn that she was still up the coast, bar bound. This meant that it would be some days before she got clear of the bar and returned to

Sydney, this was no good to me, so I collected my fare back and enquired at Sydney station about going by rail.

At that point the rail only went as far as Telegraph Pt., and I was told that all I could do was to go by train to Tenterfield and then by coach across to Casino. I would then have to book with the New England coaching Co from Casino to Woodburn. So, I bought a ticket for rail and coach to Casino via Tenterfield and boarded the train at Sydney station. There was no provision for meals aboard the train, which of course, was a steam train and the coaches were box type, no corridors. Luckily there was only one other person in my compartment, so we were able to stretch out on the seats and get some sleep. The first stop is Maitland, as far as I remember. There we were able to get sandwiches and tea.

The next one I remember was Werris Creek, where also one could have a sit-down meal of three courses for 2/- or buy sandwiches and tea. We arrived at Tenterfield early next morning, leaving the train, there were eight of us for the coach, which turned out to be a 9-seater limousine type of car. It was either a Dodge or a Wolseley, built to take eight besides the driver. Two beside the driver, three in the center and three at the back. I was seated at the back on the rear side, this coach was also the mail carrier, although there wasn't much mail and this was fastened on the offside running door track. It was rather a dusty but interesting trip as we stopped at various places along the way to put mail in

111

roadside boxes, we stopped for lunch at what appeared to be a large house, which had one room fitted up as a dining room for passengers, this was at about where Tabulam is now. The meal was quite good, and I think it was covered in the ticket price as I don't remember paying money there.

When we arrived at Casino I found that we had to stay overnight at the hotel, as the car for Woodburn left early the next morning. So, I booked my seat and returned to the hotel. Here a rather embarrassing incident occurred. On returning for the night, I found the bedroom door had no key and not being aware of the customs of the place, I put my wallet with my money in it under my pillow.

Next morning when I got up, I forgot about it and went out to the New England coach office, where they told me the hotel wanted me and to be quick as they wanted to get away. When I got to the hotel, the managers handed me my wallet and told me that people here were honest and if I thought I might be robbed, I should have left my wallet with her. I apologized and said that being a stranger I wasn't aware of the customs of the country. I offered the maid who did the room a 10/- note but she refused and said that it was her job to look out for customers. So, I learnt that in those days, most people trusted one another in the country at least, and doors weren't locked. I wish I could say as much today.

Well, I boarded the car and we got to Woodburn and there was Rita waiting at the hotel which was always where the coaches made their stops. We were both a bit shy at first and she was a little disappointed that I was not in uniform, but we soon settled down, and when I proposed booking into the hotel she wouldn't hear of it, but insisted I was to stay at her home. So, she took me along and at her house just around the next street I met her father and mother. A very nice couple, Rita's father, made me very welcome, as did her mother, who had gone to a lot of trouble to make me feel at home. Dishing up a huge meal of baked fowl, potatoes, greens, pumpkin, and sweet potato, which I tasted for the first time. This was followed with a gramma pie with lashings of thick cream, boy, that was some meal. If I'd eaten all they urged me to, I'd never have been able to get out of the chair, but I found this was the norm. Huge meals were the general run, both in the home and also in the hotels. They weren't fancy meals either and, in the hotels, quite cheap, 2/- was the most I ever paid in a hotel and often only 1/6.

So, I settled in at Woodburn and had I not had a restless nature, I'd been there yet; they certainly gave me a wonderful time. Rita took me around and showed me off to all her friends, and the people treated me like a hero. It was a bit embarrassing at times, some of the girls were very gushy, and there is no doubt many would have taken me over, had I been inclined. Then came the night of the concert, which Rita said was especially for me, by this time we had become engaged and had sent and received by Angus and Cootes by post the diamond engagement ring which cost £50, which was big money in those days and the engagement was to be announced at the concert.

It was a funny kind of affair, I found that Chris, who had been one of my friends in the 17th Batt, had also returned and was a cousin to Rita and he would also be there. When we arrived at the hall it was crowded, every person in Woodburn was there, and Bob who was by way of being the boss cocky there, was running the show, of course Woodburn wasn't a very big place in those days, only a small village in fact, but nearly every young man from there had joined up, and very many hadn't returned and so there were very few young men left. I think this accounts for the marvelous way I was accepted and treated.

Well, I found myself ushered onto the dais together with Chris, and I can tell you I was as nervous as a cat on hot bricks. Facing all those people, I couldn't keep my knees from trembling and Chris said he felt the same, but he didn't show it, after all he was a native son and I a stranger from a faraway country, but those people didn't care what I was, and they cheered and called out to me. Bob took me behind the scenes and told me that they were going to get Chris to speak first, and give me time to recover my nerve, so I must have shown how nervous I was. Rita was there and she did help me a bit, but I've never been an extravert and I haven't a clue what

Chris said but apparently, he said something about me that made them cheer like mad and he wouldn't tell me what it was, as I couldn't think of anything I'd done that was anyway remarkable or worthy of notice so I determined to get one back at him. He had been awarded the M.M for silencing a machine gun nest that had given a lot of trouble. He had crawled out into no man's land and when he got close enough, he had hurled a grenade, effectively silencing the gun and crew. He did all this under fire.

So, when they pushed me out and demanded a speech, the cheering stopped. I told them that the real hero was their own Chris, who although under heavy fire had crawled out and silenced a machine gun nest and so enabled the troops to advance.

They really went to town but when it all quieted down again, we were both seated on chairs on the dais and Bob came forward and made a short speech and announced that I had been adopted as a citizen of Woodburn and called upon Rita to come forward and present me with a gold medal, which stated that I had been adopted as a citizen of Woodburn.

When Rita had given me the medal, Bob took her by the hand and me with the other, and announced the engagement, then supper was announced, and we were mobbed. Eventually we managed to get seated and have a cup of tea and a piece of cake and of course, all the girls had to come and view the ring.

Rita's father was well to do, possessing two farms, one in Woodburn itself and the other on the south side of the river, out toward Evans Head. So, one day Rita, himself and I went out there in the sulky and he stated that this farm would be ours when we were married. We repaired some of the fencing, leaned up the house that was on the property and then home.

The house was only a two room shack really, but as he said, it was something to start with.

Actually, I wasn't in love with Rita, but I had come to like her and I sort of felt obliged to become engaged and marry her, after all, she had regularly corresponded and sent me parcels right through the two years and 77 days I was overseas, so it had sort of become taken for granted. I'd never had anything to do with women, the only other girl I ever had any affection for was my cousin Maggie, and I'd only seen her on the visits to Aunt Alice at Walthamsow. We were so much alike that we had been mistaken for twins and were the same age.

Rita was 23 and I had just turned 19 and I suppose that in a way, I conned myself into it. I just didn't know what to do and after all, it was quite pleasant to have a nice girl to make a fuss over one and be told that she loved me, but I had been brought up to regard women as something special, one always removed his hat when talking to one. Ones seat in tram, train or bus, was always vacated for a lady, and one never spoke first until spoken to.

I'm afraid I was a disappointment to Rita. I wasn't an enthusiastic fiancé, and one night we went for a walk, and she took me to the racecourse. I didn't know that that was where lovers went to make love, it was pitch dark and I couldn't see her very clearly. We sat there for about half an hour and kissed a few times. I was very uncomfortable and a little embarrassed, so after a while, I said it was getting late and we'd better get home.

She was very silent on the way home, and once she said that I was very young. I realise now that she expected me to make love to her but at that time, I hadn't a clue what to do. Oh! I did hear the troops talking about women and what they done and would do, but I still thought of women as being just a little less than angels and that the men were just being beastly and boasting. I must have been very naïve.

Well, not long after the above incident, I received a letter from Harold, who had been with me in the 17th Batt and had been sent. He had been sent home earlier and had promised me a job with him on his dairy farm and later set me up for myself. His letter asked me to come down to Singleton, as he was transferring to a new farm on the other side of the town. It did not occur to me that I did not need to leave Woodburn, that all I had to do was to marry Rita, and then start on what would have been our own farm. I had promised Harold that I would go to him on my return, and I felt obliged to keep my promise. Rita pleaded with me not to go, but I insisted that I had to keep my promise.

So, I left Woodburn in the car for Casino, where we had to change for the big nine-seater car for the trip to Tenterfield. It was at Casino that I took my first persimmon, a chap with me in the car asked me had I ever tasted them, when I said no, he went and bought a dozen and gave them to me. They were dead ripe and tasted delicious and very much like dates.

Eventually I arrived at Singleton and Harold met me with the sulky. As it was lunch time we went to the hotel for a meal and then drove out to Jersey's Plains, which is about 16 miles to the NW of Singleton on the Hunter River. Harold's grandfather had selected the property when he arrived from England, by standing on what is still known as Hobdens Hill, and taking up all the land he could see on his side of all of the Hunter River. Of course, over the years it had been cut up among all of the family. Harold's mother was an Acorn and his Aunt. Harold had decided to sell the property and with his share, settle his mother in a house in Singleton, and also to buy 'Aytondale', a property on the Northeastern side of the town, about 13 miles from Singleton at the front of the hill known as Mt Olive.

So, for a few days we collected the dairy cattle we were taking with us and loaded up the big spring cart with some furniture for his mother's house and a few farm implements. Ms. Hobden had already taken up residence in Singleton in the house she owned. I drove ahead in the cart while Harold and his uncle in the sulky, Harold being on horseback, followed behind with the cows. Arriving in Singleton at the house, we unloaded a few bits of furniture Ms. Hobden wanted, had lunch there and then set off for 'Aytondale', this had been a well-known Hereford Stud Farm before Harold bought it and had a huge barn on it and a large rambling type of house, obviously being a combination of the original old-time house, with the newer and more pretention house alongside joined by a covered way. We took over the old house, which was L shaped, consisting of a kitchen on the end, then a bedroom, then behind that a large room which had been turned into a billiard room, complete with table etc., then came the covered walk, leading to the main house. This was to be left until Harold's fiancée - a schoolteacher from Jerry's Plains - decided on the furnishing and decoration.

I stayed with Harold until July 1919. I had been at Woodburn for about six weeks, and I had often thought about the navy coming after me, after all, I had been signed on in England to do 12 or 21 years and it had cost money for my training and I couldn't see them letting me get away with it. I didn't of course realise that Australia was a huge country and I also didn't realise that now the war was over, one insignificant 1st class boy was of no more account that a flea on a rabbit, but it did nag at me occasionally and worried my conscious a bit, and although I learned to milk a cow and sit on a horse, I couldn't see that I was getting anywhere.

Although Harold had promised that he would eventually set me up with a bit of land and a few cows, I couldn't see that happening for years, and I was just an unpaid hand when it came down to tin tacks. Then there was the question of Rita, she wanted me to go back to Woodburn and get married, but I thought I'd look pretty foolish if I went back there and the navy decided to pick me up and charge me with desertion. So, I decided to take the bull by the horns and settle it once and for all. I would write and find out if they still wanted me, if they did, I'd have to make the best of it, at least they couldn't then charge me with desertion and if they didn't, I would return to Woodburn, marry Rita, and settle down. So, the letter went, Harold said I was mad, they'd forgotten all about me and wouldn't want me anyway, but he proved wrong. A week after I sent the letter, I received a warrant to travel and instructions to report to O.I.C Rushcutters's Bay. So, I wrote to Rita and told her what was happening and caught the train to Sydney.

CHAPTER TEN: PAYING OLD DUES

Arriving at the depot, I reported to a P.O in the office and he ushered me into a lieutenant. I reported myself and was sent to the medical officer. He passed me and I went back to the Petty Officer, he told me to sign some papers, which I did and I handed him my Arethusa certificate which he attached to the papers and said "you will go to Williamstown as a stoker" I said "I have been trained as a seaman, he said " you're too old, you will be a bloody stoker, stand over there". So, I stood over there and after a while he brought in three other chaps and giving me a mail warrant and meal tickets for the four of us, he said to me "you will be in charge of this party and escort them to Williamstown naval depot in Victoria and report to the S.N.R over there". Thanks to naval discipline, I did just that. It didn't occur to me that if I'd just ducked away, they probably wouldn't have bothered any further! It turned out they hadn't received any files from England.

Anyway, we arrived at Williamstown the next morning and reported it to the Master. Then we were sent to the drill hall and went through the job of collecting our kit and were given the rest of the day to get settled in. The next day I requested to see the Division Officer. He was an Australian, the only Australian officer there was at that time. I explained my situation and he was very nice but explained they had no papers about me and as I was now over 19, I would have to remain a stoker.

Being a returned soldier, I was excused squad drill, but was put in the boiler making class as a second-class stoker. This class was engaged at first on learning the rudimental's of boiler making. Our first job was to make a two-ended spanner from a piece of heavy boilerplate, first we marked out the spanner with chalk, then we had to put punch marks all around the outline, then cut through between the holes with a hacksaw and then file it to size. I found this to be quite interesting and took great care to do a good, neat job and correct for size, then I polished the whole thing up with a file and emery paper and got a commendation for it. Our next job was to make a new funnel for the 'Protector'. This was a gunboat which had disappearing guns, these guns were mounted on a sort of a spiral when they were required to fire, they rose up the spiral to the deck, fired and returned down again, or as they told me.

We had to get the boilerplate put in the rolling machine to get the proper curvations, then offset one edge, so as to take the edge of the next plate, then bore the rivet holes, heat the rivet and so fasten the plates together. This was all done under the supervision of Chief Petty Officer Stoker. When eventually we finished the funnel, we were put in the molding class. Here we had to melt various metals and make the molds out of a special black sand, having passed through this, we were given an insight into lathe work. I found this part rather boring as it mostly consisted of watching a piece of metal being turned on the lathe. Also having gone through this there was nothing much to do, also, I still thought I should be a seaman, then one day I came back from afternoon leave and found that my locker had been robbed - our lockers were like big chests- and were not locked at any time. I had a beautiful pair of Zeiss binoculars which had been taken off a dead German officer and given to me by Bill, these were gone, my return soldiers badge, medal, ribbons and Woodburn medal gone and other articles which I had kept with me over the war years, including civilian shoes.

I reported the loss to the Master, but nothing was done.

I decided that I'd had this navy and the next day I went into Melbourne and changed into civvy clothes and booked a seat on the train to Echuca. I only picked Echuca because it was the farthest point from Melbourne on the Victorian border that my money would take me. I procured a blanket, a billycan, matches, bread and cheese and set off to see something of Australia. I was already familiar with swaggies as they had often stopped at Harold's place on their journeys. I had vague ideas of walking through to Casino and then to Woodburn, this was due to the fact that when I had written to Rita and told her I was just a stoker in jumper and bellbottoms, she had broken the engagement and returned the ring, but the ring didn't look quite the same as I remembered it, and on the afternoon that my locker was rifled I had gone into Melbourne and had it valued. I went to two jewelers and they both told me they would sell me a dozen rings like that at

80/- each, so whether Angus and Coote took me down or Rita gave me another ring I'll never be certain. I did learn later from a Woodburn man at Garden Island that Rita had been engaged to a soldier that was killed at Gallipoli and that she eventually married a sailor who was either a naval cook or whose name was Cook, in any case, I only got 80/- for the ring.

I crossed the river at Echuca and was walking along the road to Deniliguin when I met up with a young, bearded chap carrying a swag and pushing a bicycle. We got talking and he said his name was Allan Faraway and his uncle owned the hotel at Deniliquin. He was only 18 but he had grown a very respectable trimmed beard, naval fashion.

He admitted that he had deserted from the navy and had been bored to death. We decided to stick together and see as much of the country as possible, so we continued on our way. It was coming on dusk, and we were debating on where we would camp for the night, we could see a light ahead and then we made for it. As we got close, we could see that the light came from a tent pitched inside the fence, which separated the road from the railway line and just then a hearty voice boomed out calling to us to come in and have a feed.

We climbed through the fence and met the owner of the voice, who turned out to be a large, dark young man of about 21 or 22. He asked no questions, just pulled up a couple of kerosene cases for seats and set to work cooking up a great pan, full of liver and bacon and eggs. Setting it out on three tin plates, he told us to tuck in. It was certainly the biggest feed of liver, bacon and eggs I'd ever eaten and incidentally, my favourite dish. After tea from the Billy, we sat around and yarned a bit.

Allan told him that he had an uncle in Deniliquin who owned the pub, and we were going there to look for work. the owner of the tent was a fettler working for the Railway and advised us that we might be able to get work on that if nothing else turned up. We unrolled our blankets and curled up for the night. In the morning at daybreak, we rolled our swags and prepared to leave, but our host insisted that we had to have breakfast first, and dished up another mighty feed of bacon, eggs, and tea. After this he shook our hands and wished us the best of luck. He obviously had some aboriginal blood, but not much and it was my first experience of Australian hospitality, and as I found later, was quite the custom among the big stations and even extended to some of the pubs who would never knock a traveler back because he had no money but might require him to cut a bit of wood for the kitchen stove.

This didn't last many more years as the real swaggies were replaced by no hopers and con men, who if they refused rations, would threaten to burn crops. That was in the days of matches, which when lit, stayed alight until burnt out. If a sundowner, as they eventually became known for their habit of arriving at a homestead just at dusk, was refused a handout, or even if the handout did not satisfy him, he would say nothing but just pull out a tin box of matches and show them as he lit a cigarette, dropping a lighted match on the ground and letting it burn out. The consequence of this was that after a few mysterious fires on places where the sundowner had been refused rations, the owners decided to take the law int their own hands and sundowners began to disappear and were never seen again, or so the story goes.

We continued our walk to Deniliquin and arrived there just on teatime or dinner, as it is called here. Allan's uncle didn't seem over enthusiastic about seeing us but gave us dinner and a room for the night. He also provided us with breakfast the next morning and the cook made us up a parcel of food to take with us and ushered us on our way. As we had no money, Allan sold his bike and we decided to make for Finlay, about 30 miles to the East. We had vague ideas of making for Queensland and to this end, we decided to walk to Sydney first, trying for work along the way and then going North from there. In those days, land in Queensland was available almost free for anyone prepared to work it, the trouble was that it was overrun with prickly pear, we poor mugs thought that all we had to do was go to Queensland, take up the land, chop out the prickly pear and then grow pineapples and bananas; we weren't the only ones imbued with this idea and quite a number of people actually tried it.

Naturally, few succeeded, until the scientists imported the cochineal insect from South America and then the situation changed as this insect got to work and in a relatively few years it's larvae cleaned up the pear and made valuable land available and Queensland, quite rightly, erected a monument for this insect.

But to continue our journey, the road to Finlay was a dirt track. The country was dry and in the grip of a drought, it was hot and dusty. Luckily, we had bought a water bag in Deniliquin, as otherwise, this would have never been written. City people don't realise just how hot and dry it can be in the back country and how quickly you would become dehydrated.

We had only walked a few miles when we had ceased to perspire and were getting very dry. Drinking from the water bag was alright but it didn't seem to quench the thirst, but we weren't too badly affected at first, like the new chums, we drank as we felt like it and soon, we had emptied the waterbag. Then we began to know what it is like to be thirsty; our sweat had dried on our shirts and left a coating of salt and so we learnt that you need a certain amount of salt to replace that lost. Up to that time, I had not done any actual stoking of a boiler, being only a trainee, so I hadn't realized the necessity of salt.

We were lucky that the government of N.S.W had built a huge tank at a place called Wollamai and a windmill kept the tank full. There was also an eastern tank or dam for stock. We were able to fill our waterbag and stomachs with water here, without this and the waterbag, we would not have made it, as we saw not a soul the whole way until we were close to Finlay. We camped at the tank that night and set off in the cool of the morning hoping to make Finlay by midday. However, when we were only three or four miles from Finlay, an old chap in a sulky met us and asked us if we wanted work, we said yes, and he told us to call in at a farm farther down the road where a farmer wanted men to stook the sheaves. We thanked him and strode on.

Eventually we came to a gate and walking in, went up to the farmhouse and enquired if they needed men. The farmer who was English said that he badly needed men to stook the wheat and would pay us £2 a week and keep. So, we went in for dinner and as neither of us had the faintest idea what stooking was, we had to find out what it was without displaying our ignorance. So! After dinner as we proceeded outside, I said to him, "some men do things one way, some another and have different methods of working, so we want to do it your way", "oh" he said, "just take the sheaves and stack them how you like, but I want a sheave on top just so" and he demonstrated with his hands.

From then on it was simple, we went to work steadily that afternoon. The sheaves of wheat had been dropped in long rows from the binder. Allan took one row and I, another. It was just a case of grabbing a sheaf in each hand, sitting them hard on the ground, butts down and leaning the heads against each other and then stacking others around the first two. When there were about 10 or 12 sheaves stacked together, you went further along and built another stook. It looked like it was easy to do, but it turned out to be hard work. The wheat was heavy and spiky, the constant bending and walking backwards and forwards, soon made itself felt and we were both tired and glad when dusk came, and we knocked off.

Returning to the house, the farmer -who's name I have forgotten-, indicated a big four-thousand-gallon tank set on the ground alongside the barn and full of water. That's the bath he said, hop in and clean yourselves up. We were still hot and dry and when we quickly undressed and hopped into the tank, which was about 3ft deep, it was a delicious bath. The water was quite warm and apparently was pumped from a bore, but it's the only time I've ever had about 3,000 gallons of water to bathe in. we found out that it was run out into the garden to irrigate the plants.

After a big dinner, he showed us to the bunk house where we camped down for the night. Next morning, we were up bright and early and after a wash from the tank, it was breakfast of steak and eggs and to work. We had been stiff and sore when we knocked off the night before, but this wore off as we got going and I rather began to enjoy the work! Morning smoko came with hot scones, cake and tea then back to work until lunch time.

The farmer was driving the reaper binder which cut the stalks at ground level and tied them into sheafs, then dropped them onto the carrier at the rear. When he had three or four sheaves on the carrier, he would press a foot lever and drop them off (today a header is used, which cuts only the heads and thrashes out the grains which is passed into the hopper) but in 1919, this farmer had only the reaper binder and he would later hire a threshing machine to thrash out the grain. So right across the paddock stretched the rows of sheaves which we were putting up in stooks. Me being always the mug, thought that we should be able to catch up to the binder. So, I suggested to Allan that we have a race and see who could get to the end of a row of sheaves first. Allan being just as dumb as me agreed, neither of us realizing that no aussie farmhand would dream of such a thing and so give ourselves away as new chums. So, we set off running from one stook to the next, trying one to beat the other.

Surprisingly, we were nowhere near so tired that night, mainly I think because the day had been much cooler and after all we were young and in very good condition. The next morning as we walked out from the house to go to work, the farmer stopped us and said that he didn't think we were worth £2 a week and keep as we were obviously new chums, and he could only pay us 30/-. I realized instantly that this was a put over, as we had really let ourselves go and because we were new chums, thought he would get away with it.

He was sadly mistaken, for I turned around instantly and said that being the case, he could pay us off now and find someone else. This took him right aback, he started to splutter a bit and said that we couldn't expect the same pay as an experienced man. I pointed out that he hadn't faulted our work or complained that we hadn't done enough, he just tried to put it over because we were new chums. I demanded our money that was 12/- each for a day and a half of work. He very reluctantly went inside and got the money and when he came out, he said if we continued working, he would make it £2.5s.

I took the money, and I started down to the gate, he watched us for a while and then followed us down and offered £2-10s a week, but I said that I wouldn't work for any man who tried to put anything over me and away we went. We walked onto Finlay, and he passed us on the road in a sulky. When we arrived in Finlay, we saw him leaving. He had not been able to get anyone and the proprietor of the hotel where we went for lunch told us that, as it was harvest time, we should have been paid casual harvest wages, which were at that time about 12/6 a day.

We decided that after all, we wouldn't walk to Sydney, but finding that we had enough to buy a rail ticket as far as Strathfield, we would walk from there if we couldn't find work there and that's what we did.

On arrival in Strathfield, we left the station and started off for Queensland. There was no work available, and we didn't think about getting a Herald and looking through its columns, so we just tramped on. We crossed the Hawksberry on a ferry and eventually arrived at Gosford. I'm a bit hazy as to just how long that took us, only a couple of days, I think. I remember getting a lift on a lorry some of the way. Our main trouble was food, by the time we hit Gosford, we were broke, couldn't find a job, and we were a bit scared of asking for food, so we just went hungry and tramped on.

At Murrindindi, a broker gave us a loaf of bread when we asked if we could chop some wood but didn't want any wood cut. We both felt a bit ashamed of this as we didn't like taking something for nothing, having both been brought up very strictly in that regard. However, on the way, past Ardglen, we passed a wheat field where shipping had been in progress and a header was standing idle in the field. It being Sunday, no-one was about, and I walked over to the header and filled my hat with wheat from the hopper, then took it back to the road. Using two stones we tried to crush it to make a porridge, but it just flew out from between the stones, so we put it in the Billy and boiled it, but it only swelled up. It did soften and we had to eat it like that, but it didn't do much to ease the hunger, and we weren't getting any fatter either, so on we trudged. I think that it was just past Willowtree that we saw a house set back off the road and Allen suggested that we go and ask for food, although very hungry, we both were reluctant to go up to the house.

Eventually we plucked up the courage and went and knocked on the door. An old lady came to the door, and I asked if we could chop some wood or do something to earn a bit of food. She told us to wait there and went back inside presently. She came back with a parcel in the newspaper and said, "you two boys have left your ship haven't you, why don't you go back instead of walking about the country?". We thanked her and went on our way, how she guessed who we were, I don't know, but Allan was a bit scared and thought that she might put the police onto us. I said she was only guessing and how could she get the police even if she wanted to? We decided to follow the railway line and near a settlers shed; we saw a rail trike. Allan said that if we took this, we could go a long way without walking, he had apparently had a temporary job on the Victorian Railways at one stage. So, we took the trike and I sat on top of our swags and Allan pulled the trike.

This was a bit uncomfortable for me as I had to keep my legs up off the ballast, at one stage we had a long run downhill. We must have gone quite a long way on the trike before we came to a steep hill, we had passed through Werris Creek with me walking outside the line carrying the swags, whilst Allan boldly pulled the trike right through, apparently no-one was about, it being Sunday and we walked the trike up the hill until in a cutting near the top. Allan said to get on again, we had just gone around a curve in the cutting when a loud whistle right behind us made me jump off the trike and there, right behind us was the engine of a goods train, we hadn't thought about trains, and it was lucky it was uphill.

Allan kept his head and pulled the trike off the line. The driver and fireman asked if we were alright, Allan waved and said we were ok, and the train went on. Just around the corner was a small platform unattended and we pulled the trike off the line there and decided to camp for the night. There didn't seem to be any habitations about, it seemed to be in the middle of the bush, so we unrolled our swags in the shed on the platform. There was a flock of sheep in the paddock adjoining the line and one sheep had pushed through the wire and got tangled. Allan said, "how about some chops for tea?", I said "they'd hang us if they caught us". Allan said "who's to know and we were almost starving anyway, so we got the sheep and Allan very dexterously cut its throat and skinned it.

We buried the fleece in a hole behind the platform
and retaining the two hind legs, the liver and
kidney, we buried the rest with the fleece. We
roasted the legs and using the fat around the kidneys
and old kerosene tin we managed to fry the liver and
kidneys and give ourselves a feed. I'm still a bit
hazy as to the length of time that it took us to travel
from Strathfield to Tamworth, but it must have been
some time.

CHAPTER ELEVEN: PUNISHMENTS FOR WAYWARDING

After leaving the place where the sheep was caught,
we trudged on towards Tamworth and I decided that
when we reached Tamworth, I'd give up and go
back to the navy. The game just wasn't worth the
candle, there seemed to be no jobs available that we
could do; this was 1919, and thousands of returned
me were probably in a similar plight. We were
heroes when we were away but a problem when we
returned, and no-one told us that the federal
government was preparing an apprenticeship
training scheme for chaps like myself, when I found
that out it was too late.

On arrival in Tamworth, I went to the local branch
of the Returned Soldiers League, of which I was
still a member. I showed my discharge, explained
our situation, and asked for help to get back to

Sydney. They promptly supplied us with an order for food to the value of 10/- and provided me with a single fair ticked to Sydney. Allan, not being a returned soldier, gave himself up to the police and I never came across him again. I believe he fared better than me, as I heard that he'd only been fined, and leave stopped on arrival in Sydney. I reported to Garden Island and was placed under close arrest, which meant that I was confined to the island. This wasn't too bad at first since Mick was the Petty Officer Quartermaster and after reporting to the Officer of the Day, I was allowed to mess with the men and wander through the island. One could then only leave by ferry and the guards were at the ferry pontoon to see that I didn't leave.

Commodore G was the officer commanding the island which was designated HMAS PENGUIN. Then one day I was taken before him and he gave me a dressing down, saying I was a disgrace to the Royal Navy and should have set an example to these Australians, so I was to be punished by Royal Warrant. Next Saturday morning at 9 am all the ship's crew, that is all the naval personnel, were mustered to divisions. I was marched out in front of the men, the warrant was read out by the Commodore, and I was stripped of all my colour, silk and lanyard and sentenced to 30 days detention with hard labour. I then marched to the detention quarters which then occupied one end of the island behind the church building.

The prison, for that's what it really was, consisted of two tiers of cells, Lower Floor and Upper Floor. I was No 12 on the Upper Floor and on entering the building, I was placed immediately in front of the Chief Master at Arms officer, behind me were the stairs leading to the upper corridor cells, to my left was a wall with a door in the left-hand corner leading to the kitchen. In the right-hand corner was the door to the lower cell, in between on that wall was a large glass fronted case, over the top of the case in big black letters was the word SILENCE. In the case were one set of leg irons, one pair of handcuffs and one straight jacket.

The Chief Master at Arms was a huge man, Warrant Officer Holley, he always roared at the top of his voice and he now said to me "offender, do you see that sign?" pointing to the word above the case, "yes Sir" I replied "silence you scum, speak when you are spoken to, and answer Yes Sir or No Sir and nothing else, do you understand", then to the Petty Officer Instructor, - they didn't call them wardens – "put him in 12". I was marched up the stairs through an iron grille to No 12 cell. When the grille was opened the bolt is slammed back with force to make the maximum noise, the same on opening and closing the cell doors. However, the instructors never themselves open the cell door if that cell is occupied, but instead they unlock the big chubb locks, slam back the bolt and refasten the lock.

Then they retreat to the grille at the end of the corridor and roar out "Upper Corridor stand by your room door", on this command the occupant doubles to his door and places the palm of his hands on the inside of his door, then on the command "outside your room" he doubles out and around, pushing the door so that it just touches the wall with him facing it and woe betide him if the door clangs when it touches the wall.

My hammock had been taken from me, and I was told my behavior would determine when I got it back. My kitbag I had to stow on the small white wood rack in the right-hand corner of the cell. The cells were 10 ft long by 6 ft wide, in the right-hand corner was the rack to hold the kitbag, in the other corner were two whitewood boards each 6 ft by 18 inches by 2 inches. These were rested on two L shaped irons set in the wall and floor. On these against the wall was a wooden box with a sloped top to serve as a pillow, it was 2 ft 6 inches long, about 6 inches wide, about 1 inch or so thick in the front and about 2 inches at the back. On the front wall beside the door, two angle irons set in the wall held a little whitewood table about 24 x 18 inches or less, on this rested a bible and an aluminum basin. In the corner near the table was an aluminum bucket which was an all-purpose toilet and scrub bucket. So, on the Saturday before Christmas 1919, I found myself in Garden Island naval jail.

At lunch time 12 noon the command came "Upper Corridor stand by your room door" then "outside your room" then "upper corridor right and left, turn and march" and we doubled down the stairs and collected our lunch or more probably dinner. I received a tin plate on which was 8 oz of bread and 4 oz of meat. We doubled back upstairs and to our cells, we then, one at a time, doubled to the end of the corridor to collect a small basin of water, then locked in our cells. I couldn't eat the dry bread so I climbed on the bed boards and put it through the bars of the one small window, thinking the birds would eat it. However, at 12:30 one instructor Bob came to my cell and said, "A bloody fine Arethusa boy you've turned out to be, do you think you could use a palm and a needle?". Had he not used a bullying tone of voice I would have probably said yes but instead, I said no. he roared "you're a bloody liar, do you think you're the only Arethusa boy in the world and call me sir when I speak to you", then he spotted the bread "and so the food's not good enough for you?". I said "No, Sir" and he roared at me not to answer him back. I promptly told him where to go, to which was a stupid thing to do as he promptly said "Right, a bit cocky are you, well we'll soon cut you down to size, for a start, no library books this week-end and dry rations only".

With that he slammed out of the cell, but later came back with the Chief Master of Arms who took the bread from the window and said that he would give me one more chance, if I didn't eat what was given to me, then I would get none until I did, moreover, there was a strait jacket and leg irons waiting for obstinate offenders:, and with that he went out. A little while after, Wyburn came back and opened the cell door, threw in a coal sack and a length of tarred rope. He told me to get to work and rope up the bag, he called No 14 from his cell and stood by while No 14 explained to me how to sew the rope around the bag, so as to leave two handles, one on each side of the sack.

This meant that one had to splice the two ends of the rope together in a short splice, and the rope sewn onto the bag with the splice at the bottom and he whispered to me that I was expected to splice and sew 2 ½ bags a day, even on Sunday and although our ½ hour meal breaks were supposed to be free, yet he said the only way to get them done was to work while you ate. This puzzled me at first because I couldn't see how roping 2 ½ sacks would take so long, especially since I later finished the one, I was doing before tea time came. This consisted of 4 oz of bread and ½ pint of milk and immediately I got this, I was given another sack to do, which by the way, I never did finish, for when lights out came the bag was taken away and never came back.

The next day was Sunday and at 6 am we were called out and doubled down to the yard and given half hour of physical jerks, then back to the cells, on the way collected breakfast, which consisted of our own small bowls half filled with a porridge of cornmeal, unsweetened with some milk and 4 oz of dry bread. I was hungry enough by this time to eat the porridge and dry bread without any trouble. After we had been let out one at a time to wash our bowls, we were loaded up in our cells.

I forgot to mention that when Revielle went at 6 am, we had to be let out of our cells to empty our slop bucket and collect a dish of water, with this we had to wash ourselves, scrub the bed boards and kitbag, small table and then wash the floor and clean out the bucket. This had to be done in 15 minutes.

To my surprise, no bags were brought to my cell to be roped, instead Chief Petty Officer Instructor, who was known as Robbo, came to my cell, came in and shut the door, sat on the edge of the bed boards, looked me up and down and then said quietly "you've been giving yourself a bit of trouble, haven't you" I said "yes sir" then he said "in among ourselves you call me Robbo, but outside or if any other instructors are present I'm a real bastard, you understand?", "yes sir" I replied "right, can you use a palm and needle, that is not as you do on the bags but sailmakers way?", I said "yes sir", "right, I'll see you after church" he replied.

At 10 am we were mustered in the yard and doubled through the corner door up some stairs and into the balcony of the church, the church was the old Sail Loft of Sailing ship days and had been converted to a church. We were up on the balcony behind a screen mesh so we couldn't be seen from the body of the church.

After church we went back to our cells and collected our dinner which consisted of 4 oz of meat, 4 oz of potatoes, and 4 oz of bread. After dinner Robbo came into my cell with a yard of 18-inch-wide canvas, a sail hook, palm, needle, knife and a book. "Right" he said "I want you to table both sides of this canvas, when you finish that, you can read the library book. So, I spent part of Sunday afternoon turning over and stitching down the sides of the canvas. I tied the corner of the sail hook to the leg of the Angle iron and with the hook itself to hold the canvas taught, it was easy to double over and stitch down the edges. I took care to make neat even stitches since no marking wheel was used. The book was 'Mr. Midshipman Easy' by Captain Marryat. I never quite finished it, as at lights out Robbo came and collected the canvas and the book.

Next morning at 6 am – here I must mention that when lights out went we had to strip off and place our clothes, neatly folded on the floor in front of the door and we lay on the bare boards with one blanket and nothing else, so you could see that we had to move very smartly to get dressed in singlet and trousers, wash, scrub bed boards, rack, table and bucket in the ¼ hour allotted and be standing by the door. Punishments included no library book, extra work, cutting down rations, and if necessary, solitary confinement in strait jacket. Only one of the instructors was a stickler for rules, he was a short fat leading Seaman, who's name I've forgotten, and he rarely did a shift on the cells, he did a yard i.e., the three men on barrow duty and morning physical jerks. The other two first class P.O Bob and Sid with Chief P.O Robinson did the cell duties plus, gun loading on the dummy gun and Swedish drill in the shed on the wall ladders.

So, on this Monday morning we did our regular physical jerks in the yard, then after breakfast, we ate the usual cornmeal and bread. We doubled down to the yard and three men were detailed for loading practice, three men on the wall ladders, three men on the barrows at the boiler plates and double post, and the remainder four I think to Swedish drill in the after part of the shed. I was allotted to the big steel barrow at the double post, ahead of me was the 1st boiler plate (which had a great heap of 3 inch blue metal on it) was No 14, on the No 2 BP was No 10 opposite me, and the Leading Seaman bellowed "on the word go, No 14 will commence shovelling metal into his barrow, at the same time No 12 will double with his barrow to take the place of No 14, No 10 will double round to take No 12's place. Now I want to see you move and I want that metal shifted from No 1 plate to No 2 plate in double quick time and double that shovel, ready Go!".

Now I must explain that the barrows were simply so heavy for me that I could only stagger with it, and it had a very strong tendency to tip over. This with the Leading Seaman yelling for me to get a move on got me mad and when I reached the boiler plate with the metal and stopped to pick up the No 4 shovel.I threw the shovel down and told the LS to load the bloody metal himself.

Boy! Did that cause a stir, all worked stopped, whistles blew and before you could say Jack Robinson, Bob and Sid were there with truncheons and I found myself grabbed by the arms, rushed through the yard gate, up the stairs and into the cell. My kitbag, rack, bed boards, table and bible were all taken out and I was locked in the bare cell. So, I sat on the bare stone floor and prepared myself for whatever may happen. The next thing was "No 12, on your feet" but I sat where I was and the door was flung open and the person came in. he told me to stand up but I said that I was quite comfortable where I was, then he said that I was an unreasonable and stupid boy and that I should do as I was told, that it was my Christian duty to accept my punishment and go back to work. I told him what I thought of his Christianity and to get out and leave me alone. Next Chief Holly came and threatened me with all sorts of punishments, but I took no notice, and he left and locked me in. at no time was I touched to my surprise as I half expected to be beaten up, but when teatime came, I was given 4 oz of dry bread and 1 pint of water.

Next morning, I was left in my cell, having slept on the floor with only my clothes, singlet and no blanket, luckily it was summer and not too cold in the stone cell. At 9 am came the command "No 12, stand by your room door", which I did, the door was unbolted then "outside your room" then "left turn", it was Sid, he said very quietly "don't be foolish, take it steady", I nodded, then "at the double downstairs". I was then ushered into a room

144

adjoining the office, which had a communicating door. I was given my jumper and cap and told to put them on, which I did.

Then the communications door was opened, and I marched in to see Commodore Glassop sitting at the table with my file in front of him. Then he looked through my file, glanced up and said, "so you refused duty", I replied "no sir, I only refused to do stupid useless work, that I didn't mind doing anything constructive, but I objected from stripping metal from one plate to another, for no useful purpose".

He heard me out and then said, "it's not for you to say what you should do, that is a part of the punishments, do you realise that I can give you 90 days for refusing duty", "yes sir, but I understand that at the end of the 90 days I have to be given 48 hours free and I intend on that case to go to the press and tell them how men are treated here", "do you threaten me?", 'no sir, I'm just stating facts, even convicts weren't asked to shift metal for nothing". He looked at me for what seemed quite a while, then he said, looking through my file "you were trained on the Arethusa", "yes sir", "you were trained as a seaman and the chief here tells me that you obviously are", "yes sir, I tried to tell them at Rushcutters Bay, but they took no notice", "so I see" he said "I also see that you have good marks in your stokers training", "yes sir", "are you aware that you were signed on for 12 years with the Royal Navy", "yes sir, 12 or 21", "quite so but only 6 years here", "yes sir", "of course you understand that we could require you to serve the original if the R.N decided to claim you", "yes sir and I'm quite prepared to do that sir", "very good, I propose to give you another chance, you will go back and do your duty, and if you behave yourself at the end of the original 30 days, you will return to Williamstown, now I am very short of A.B's it seems to me that a lad with your training is wasted as a stoker, so I propose if the board of Admiralty agree that on your return to Williamstown that you make applications to your Commanding Officer to transfer to the Executive Branch, on which you will be rated as Ordinary Seaman to give you the opportunity to brush up on your seamanship, at the end of six months you should have no trouble being rated A.B, and indeed I should be surprised if you do not qualify for leading rate. I've been very fair with you, and you are getting off very lightly, so let's have no more nonsense and go back to duty". Then the chief "On caps, about twin double march" and so I went back to my cell.

The bed boards were replaced, as was the table but not the kit bag or rack, my jumper and cap were removed. I was officially put on punishment rations. Breakfast 1 pint of water, 8 oz of bread. Dinner 4 oz meat, 4 oz potato, 4 oz bread, or 4 oz meat, 8 oz bread. Tea 4 oz meat, 1 pint of water.

Then Robbo came to the cell "you got off fairly well considering, good job you were trained for the R.N: now can you mark out for sails?" I said "I think so",

146

"do reef points and cringles", "yes sir", "right, now you will do the early morning physical jerks but after tomorrow you will not go down in the yard again after breakfast, instead I will come and take you down to the yard, there we will do some marking out and then I will tell you what you are to do savvy", "yes sir". So, he left me on my own, I realized that in the punishment diet, I wouldn't be able to wheel metal or do gun loading, or the very strenuous Swedish drill on the bars and wall ladders, but the light early morning physical drill would be sufficient to keep me fit.

I am sure that Glassops was completely unimpressed with my threat about going to the press, but it may have alarmed the Naval Staff Board as had the punishments as carried out at Garden Island, been featured, and made public, there would have been quite a furor. As it was next morning I went to the physical drill, but after breakfast when all the other prisoners were about their various jobs, Robbo appeared with a large bolt of canvas and a blue pencil. Taking me down to the yard we unrolled it, marked out for a pair of cutter rig sails, we marked out the reef points and cringle places then back to the cell. I was given a pair of sailmakers shears, needles and twine, sail hook, knife, palm, and the reef points. These are merely lengths of cord which are shamrocked and stitched onto the sail in that shape along the reefing line.

On arrival in the cell Robbo said "you're on your own now. You've got the rest of your 30 days to do the job, so take your time and make it good". So, for the next 27 days that's what I did, physical jerks first thing, then the sails for the rest of the day. I never got my hammock back until the day I left, meanwhile, I folded my singlet and trousers every night and placed them before the door and slept naked under the one blanket. Then came Christmas, I heard the sirens of the ships and then a break.

I think it was either New Year's Eve or a day after New Year, we were all jumpers, caps and boots and mustered in the yard. We were issued with rifle and bayonet and drawn up in a line. I was placed on the extreme right acting as marker and on the command "fix bayonets". I had to take two smart paces forward and taking their time from me place left hand on bayonet half, whip it from the scabbard and hold it straight out in front of me so all could see, then place it smartly on the rifle muzzle, then two quick paces back and all at attention. Then the door from the church opened and a procession of Brass Hats emerged with Glassop, a Rear Admiral, a Vice Admiral, a Captain and I think a Lieutenant Commander.

Then came the order "offenders slope arms, offenders present arms" very nicely done for the officers saluted, and then "order arm" back to the slope, across the body for attention at the orders, also nicely done, heads erect, eyes front, don't move a muscle, the Brass advanced on us and Glassop and the Vice Admiral stopped in front of me, and said "this is the man I mentioned sir" me, wondering what the hell this was all about stared straight ahead. The Admiral "your name", "honey, sir", "Arethusa boy", "yes sir", "carry on" and that was that. When the Saturday morning of my discharge came, I was given back my cap, jumper, collar, silk and lanyard and paraded before Glassop. He said I had proved his trust and had done well and informed me that the Navy board had approved of my transfer to the Executive Branch, that he couldn't make me transfer but hoped that I would have the good sense to see where my best interests lay and apply for the transfer as soon as I reached Williamstown.

I've never understood why he didn't get me to make the application then had he done so I would have signed it and my whole life probably changed, perhaps he considered it would have been going over the head of the Williamstown commander, anyway, he didn't and after he dismissed me I was paraded in front of Chief Hotley, and of course he asked me if I was going to transfer, out of pure devilment, knowing he was all bluff and bluster, I said I might transfer to be a cook, "Cook" he roared "you couldn't cook a bloody egg", "oh" I said "I don't know, I've cooked eggs before", "Don't give me any of your insolence, you're not out of here yet", so I said no more and was escorted outside just in time for lunch at the mess.

CHAPTER 12: TIME SERVED

That was January 3rd, 1920, a Saturday, and on the 6th I, with two others and a Leading Seaman were sent by train back to Williamstown, the other two men were recruits. Arriving there we reported to the Master at Arms and then I was sent to the Chief Regulating Stoker. I was told that I was to be drafted to the Australia but as she was at sea I had to stand by and wait until it was convenient to send me. So, from then until 5th of February I was given various jobs, first as the gunner's mate in the armory where I had to look after, keep clean and issue out as required various pistols and rifles. Then I had a spell helping Leading Stoker Joe Sefton (his uncle was Hoyt's manager in Melbourne) and Joe had persuaded Commander Keighly that it was a good idea to have a film unit for entertainment purposes, this was approved by the Navy Board and Joe was given a special rating as a film specialist. He asked for me to be seconded to him as assistant and this was agreed to as a temporary measure. We were given a room on the ground floor of the barracks and Joe set up his gear there. He used to go to Melbourne and his uncle lent him a projector, motor and films and we used to have to run them through to make sure they were all right, and then rewind them, ready for the nightly show, in consequence, I saw a lot of films that I otherwise would have not seen. The trouble was we had the room darkened with a screen at one end and every now and then some inquisitive rating, hoping to get a look, would open the door and disturb the whole thing, besides making a darn nuisance of themselves. Now joe was a fully qualified electrician, and he solved the problem by connecting a wire from the motor to the door handle and while not lethal, it gave a nasty shock and that would have finished the prying, only one morning we were running a film through when the Commander Darley knocked at the door and then grabbed the handle to open it. He took it very well considering but Joe had to disconnect the wire. Darley, who was the only Australian officer we had at the time, issued strict orders that we were not to be interrupted and that worked (he was later killed in China, a real officer, and gentlemen).

Eventually on the 5th of February 1920 a number of us were mustered with our kitbags and hammocks and were marched to Spencer Street station and entrained to Sydney where we arrived the next morning and boarded H.M.A.S Brisbane, at Garden Island as passengers to Australia. She sailed that day to Jervis Bay; we passengers did the dirty work of hauling ashes from the stokehold lifts to the ships side and dumping them overboard.

While at Jervis Bay, we amused ourselves fishing and before long we were hauling in mackerel by the hundred, we arranged for the cooks to fry them for dinner and all would have been well, only some silly coot of a seaman made some derogatory remark to a stoker, this developed into a free for all brawl. We stokers were winning easily, using the mackerel as ammunition, but the seaman brought a hose into operation, and we being on the mess deck below the seaman couldn't then get at them, so we had to surrender after getting well and truly drenched.

CHAPTER THIRTEEN: BOARDING 'THE AUSTRALIA'

We arrived in Hobart early morning of the 7th of February 1920 and were marched aboard the Australia (this was the battle cruiser of 1914-18 war) and reported aboard to the commander who paraded us to the Captain, Claude, then to Chief Regulating Stoker who allocated us our duties. I was paired with Bill, and we of course became mates, always worked together, and went about together. The Aussie, as we called her, had 31 boilers in five stokeholds, or more properly Boiler rooms, and used both coal and oil and could do 31 knots, if necessary, carried eight 12-inch guns in four turrets, she had twin rudders and three screws or propellors. Bill and I were at first put in the first part of the red or port watch, our job when on watch was to keep the coal up to the boilers, at each end of the boiler room and on each side were the coal bunkers and oil tanks, there were also reverse bunkers overhead of the end and side bunkers.

Our job when steaming was to fill the steel skips, which were on runners, run them down the floor plates and tip the coal in a line in front of the boilers.

The Aussie didn't get much sea time, we found later that under the Versailles treaty, she was to be scrapped. We did not get ashore in Hobart at that time as we sailed the next morning and returned to Sydney, here we went into Ley dock at Cockatoo Island. This was quite an interesting performance as owing to her size being over 900 ft long and drawing 35 ft to waterline, there was only just room for her to fit in. She was pushed by two tugs at the stern and a huge steel cable from her bow to a winch at the head of the dock pulled her in. When they closed the lock gates there was only 6 inches underneath. Nevertheless, she was propped up with great timber baulks. All hands were to take 42 days leave but a working party of stokers were to be left aboard to keep one boiler room for steam and dynamo for the bathhouse and kitchen. I volunteered for the stoker party together with Petty Officer Stoker Ward and another chap Anderson. One cook and one officer comprised the caretaker party and we were told that we could get our 42 days leave later.

It was an easy job to keep one boiler going, as it wasn't under forced draught and at night, we simply banked the fires. The boilers were 'Babcocks and Wilcocks' water tube boilers and had four doors to each fire, these were numbered and when steaming under forced draught with 200 lb. psi. The firing rate was governed by the Kilroy indicator, there was one on each side of the boiler room and were controlled by the engine room, who set them to ring according to the steam pressure as shown in the Engine Room.

So, if we were just using cruising speed it would only ring about every three or four minutes, but if we were steaming full speed, or the guns were operating then they'd ring almost every minute, and one would be flat out keeping up with it as each stoker on his stoker had to swing the his fire door for the one next to him and they had to be fired alternatively. First 1, then 3, then 2, then 4 and the coal had to be spread evenly over the surface of the fire. This was a knack required by experience. As your mate swung the door open, you landed your shovel of coal on the fore plate and with a little twist, the coal would fly in and spread over the fire. You then immediately turned and grabbed the appropriate door handle of your mate's boiler and he would send his shovel full into his fire.

As you can see, when steaming full speed or firing the guns, one was running flat out to keep up speed. The oil burners were only used if the steam couldn't be maintained at the 200 lb mark and that was very rare. With all this, one fire had to be cleaned each watch. To do this, one had to use the big slice to break up the clinker and rake it out in front of the boiler. This was hot work as the coals fell right at your feet, then the rake was used to bring burning

154

coal from alongside the part raked out, and then more coal fed in. this had to be done without letting the pressure fall below 160 psi, neither must it go over the 200 psi, as then it would blow off through the safety valve and that meant dire punishment. One learns very quickly under those conditions, and you can believe they get quite hectic. We had a good Petty Officer, and he would sometimes help out if things looked like they were beating us, but back to the dock. We had a very easy time while on the dock, we kept the fire in the boiler banked just sufficiently to keep 100 lb. of steam and banked right up at night.

Our hardest job was when we had to clean the boiler out, we had to do this when we had too much clinker on the plate, then we lit another boiler and when it was working properly we cleaned the old one right out and swept the slopes and tubes, a filthy job, and put all the clinker in coal bags, carted them up in the lift, across the gang plank and stowed them on the dock. The rest of the time, we watched the dock yard matey's or went fishing from the ferry pier.

Eventually the Captain and crew all returned from leave and things were made shipshape again. One of the things they did in the dock was to take all the big watertight doors, these doors had three dogs' clips on each side, two top and bottom. This meant that when closing the door in an emergency there were ten dog clips to knock around to make the door watertight. So, they welded six inches of plate all the way around and then fitted smaller doors which could be clamped fast by one center lever. This would have made sense in active service, but since she was to be scrapped and then sunk, it was a sheer waste of time, money, and labour, anyway, more on that later.

Naturally Ward, Anderson and I expected to get our 42-day leave, but nothing happened. Anyway, the Prince of Wales, Edward, was due here and so we pulled out of the dock and eventually took off together with the destroyers, Parramatta, Swan and Torren for rendezvous with H.M.S Renown in Perth. Bill and I had been rated first class stokers by this time and we had volunteered for auxiliary watch keeping. This meant that when in harbour we had our two boilers and two trimmers, and we worked 6 hours on and 6 hours off in 24 hours. Two trimmers from the starboard watch relieved us, so we did two 6 hour watches every second day and then had 24 hours off when we could go ashore. Our two trimmers were second class stokers Trevena and Harvey, Ward was our P.O. We liked this arrangement for we could go ashore immediately when we finished our last watch and have a whole day ashore.

Of course, on our day off the second part of the port and starboard watch auxiliary workers did the same. The catch in it, as we quickly found out, was when we put to sea and found that we still worked 6 hours on 6 off, but every day with no day off. The reason being of course that with only two boilers being used, all 31 were operating and this required all hands

On this trip to escort the Prince, we were to have gone into Melbourne to pick up our sea plane but the weather turned really bad, so much so that even the old Aussie rolled like a drunken sailor. The captain signaled the destroyers to go into Melbourne, but we continued across the Bight and boy was she rough! The Aussie, with most of her weight below water, sort of rolled from the bottom like a pendulum and this made it hard for both us and the trimmers. On one watch the ashpits and floor plates were awash and when I went to stoke my fires Bill would have to hang onto my belt with one hand while swinging the fire door with the other, and I had to do the same for him., This was one occasion when oil was also fed in through the burners. The trimmers had the worst of it as they had to hang onto the ship while they were filling it, and then hang on like grim death to stop it breaking away from them as they pushed it along the plates. On one occasion, they had just filled the skip when it got away just as the ship rolled away from them, and it skidded down the room with water sloshing about.

Chief Petty Officer Hepplewhite had just come around the forward boiler and was standing looking up at the Kilroy indicator when it caught him square behind the knees, luckily just before it hit him the ship had started to roll the other way, so it didn't have its full force. Moreover, he was standing relaxed with knees slightly bent to cancel the rolling movement, even so he sat down on the skip pretty hard and was well bruised. He was lucky his legs hadn't broken but he certainly hadn't hurt his voice. He was quite vocal about silly so and so's who couldn't manage a skip in a little bit of a seaway, but it really was a very bad storm, so much so that the skipper hove too. In consequence, we didn't meet Renown as planned, she beat us into Freemantle where we tied up behind her.

Bill and I had a trip ashore where we made the acquaintance of two nurses from Kenmore mental hospital. They spoke to us just as we were about to enter a picture theatre. One of them was about 22 and very nice looking. Bill cottoned onto her and left me to the other woman who was a good deal older, but a very nice person just the same. They offered to show us around Freemantle and Perth. Bill accepted right away, I wasn't so keen myself but couldn't very well back out, so went along. As it turned out it was a very enjoyable afternoon. They showed us the Kings gardens and the sights of the town including the shopping arcade which is a copy of a piece of old London.

We were still on Auxiliary watch-keeping and had to be on watch at 4 bells, 6 pm, so we returned, Bill was engaged to a very nice girl in Melbourne but seemed to have fallen for the young nurse, they had asked us to meet them again, but Bill managed to make a swap and got away the next day. Then we got our 24-hour leave and Bill went off with the young nurse and left us. We went to the pictures and then not being much of a ladies' man, I told the nurse that I had to get back aboard. I spent the rest of the day in the canteen on the wharf, run by a ladies' welfare committee, watched the concert then aboard ready for the 12 – 6 am watch.

On our next day off I received a note asking the two of us to meet the nurses near the G.P.O as we were sailing the next day. Bill and I had been cleaning the slopes and funnel the day before and had climbed to the top of the funnel inside and were looking down at the crowds on the wharf. Bill had been seen by the officer of the watch and was promptly logged and his next day's leave stopped. So, I went on my own and met the nurses. I told them that Bill had been logged and they said that they wanted to give us a little send off, so had arranged a little luncheon for us. They took me downstairs to a quiet little restaurant, where we had a very nice lunch, which they insisted on paying for. The young one was very keen on knowing about Bill, she obviously had fallen for him very hard, but of course I couldn't say anything except that he was my watch mate. They asked me to write and keep in touch, I wrote once from Hobart later but never heard from them again.

We sailed the next day and eventually arrived back in Sydney, where a huge crowd had gathered around Farm Cove to welcome us in. it must have been an impressive sight from the shore, the two big battle cruisers, Renown in the lead with the Prince's

Standard at the fore, then the Brisbane, Melbourne and Sydney with the six river class destroyers.

I couldn't see it as I was on watch luckily, as it gave me first day ashore. The Prince came and went and Anderson and I were still waiting for our leave. On the 1st of May I made an application for my leave, but the chief put me off, he said that they couldn't let me go until the reserve bunkers had been cleared. These were two huge bunkers which stretched over the engine room right aft to the stern and were filled with coal that had been there from the first days of the war. I didn't know then that they were emptying the ship to be ready for the scrap yard. I could see that I'd be lucky if I even got the leave, so Chris and I put our heads together and decided to take our leave and chance the consequences. So on my next day off, the 5th of may I think, we went ashore and caught a train to Singleton with the intention of staying at Harold overnight and then walking to Queensland and Brisbane, but unfortunately for us, Constable Small, who knew me, had seen me in uniform the couple of times I had visited Harold on weekend leave he saw us but did nothing, he couldn't do anything until after we had overstayed our leave. Nevertheless, he apparently made it his business to contact Newcastle or Sydney as we found later.

We walked to Aytondale, Harold's place at Mt Olive, he of course was quite surprised but greeted us ok and asked me was I on leave. So, I told him that I was taking leave, he didn't like this and said I could only stop there for the night as he wasn't going to be involved, so I told him we'd leave in the morning. He told us that the only room he had was taken by the lad that he had employed in my place, but we could sleep in the corn shed. He had married the schoolteacher, but she said not a word, I asked Harold if my uniforms were still here, he asked if I wanted them and I said yes, that we couldn't stay away and still wear naval uniform but there were still plenty of returned men still wearing and working in their uniforms.

To go back, I must explain that on going to Woodburn on discharge from the army, I had packed my uniforms consisting of 1 pair of riding breeches, 1 pair khaki slacks, 1 tunic, 1 dungaree coat, leggings and hats into my kitbag and left them with the Seamans mission on going to Harold's. I had just gone to Sydney on my return ticket, picked up the kitbag and left it at Harold's place when I went back into the Navy, and this was what I asked for now. He grudgingly said that he couldn't stop me from taking them, I said he could have the kitbag, all I wanted was the tunic, dungaree coat and slacks and bridges.

I began to realise that he was no mate to rely on and I remembered that when he had been placed on draft for France he had complained of bad feet and in fact he had been found to be flat footed. He had then been given a job in the regimental Post Office but had been sent home. I still didn't think he would do anything against me, and he did give us a feed. So,

161

we slept in the corn shed that night and at the first break of dawn we crept out and divided the uniforms between us. I wore the tunic and slacks and Chris the dungaree coat and breeches. I didn't realise what a queer looking pair we were but putting the naval uniforms in the kitbag we set off not back to Singleton but across country towards Muswellbrook. Harold had the phone on and when he discovered us gone phoned the police of Singleton and to cover the reason for ringing them up, and so he wouldn't be charged with aiding and abetting us, he said we had stolen his uniforms, which is something he didn't have, moreover, they wouldn't fit him as he was much bigger than me.

Anyway, not knowing this at the time, we trudged over hills and valleys towards Muswellbrook. As we climbed one hill, we passed a farmhouse and all the family came out to look at us. They seemed to be frightened when I asked if we were on the right road, of course we didn't know that Small had contacted all the farms with phones and told them to watch out for us but not to stop us as we might be dangerous. So, we went on and eventually at one place near the rail line, which we could see at the bottom of the hill, we saw a light in a house. We knocked at the door and asked if we could camp in the barn for the night, he had of course been warned that we were heading that way, but if he thought we were dangerous, he didn't show it. He made us welcome and got a good feed of steak and eggs with bread and butter and showed us into two single beds for the night.

We were dead tired after our long walk and slept like logs. The old chap of course got on the phone and told the police that he had us there. They told him to leave us, and they would collect us in the morning. I was told this by the constable who escorted me later to Sydney. However, we got up real early in the morning and would have gone on our way, but the old chap got up too and insisted on cooking us a huge breakfast of bacon and eggs with toast, butter, and jam. He was trying to keep us there until the police arrived, but we didn't know that we didn't waste time and as he wouldn't take any money we left and continued on our way. I had become increasingly uneasy about the way that people looked at us and I said to Chris that it might be a good idea to change back into uniform before we reached Muswellbrook.

We had now reached the main road and were walking along it when a mounted constable rode towards us and pulled up, hitching his pistol around so we could see it. He asked where we were making for, we told him Muswellbrook. He said that he would go along with us and that he might be able to get a lift for us, we hadn't gone another 100 yards when a car came tearing up with a police sergeant and two more constables in it. They all jumped out and the sergeant said "You, the two lads from the Navy" I said, "Yes why?", he said "you better come with me", so we got in the car, and he drove us to Muswellbrook, when we got to the station he told us to change into our uniforms, which we did. Then he asked me if these army uniforms were the ones that

I stole from Harold", I said we stole nothing, that they were my own uniforms and they wouldn't fit Harold anyway, that he didn't object to me taking them and he knew they were mine. "Well," he said, "I believe you but it's not my pigeon, they will deal with that at Singleton". So, we got back in the Car and the sergeant drove us to Singleton and handed us over to Constable Small, who was also the goaler. We were then searched and our belongings taken and entered into the book, then Small insisted that we had to be fingerprinted. I said "I haven't committed any crime and I haven't been tried, you have no right to take our fingerprints" but he insisted and since I had no intention of getting into conflict with the law, I let him take them.

In the afternoon we were taken into the courtroom before a J.P who happened to be the stepfather of Harold's friend who was also ex 17th Batt. I think his name was Milligan. I don't know what the JP's name was, Steve and Harold were both there, but they said nothing and were asked nothing. The J.P said "you are charged with stealing two uniforms, the property of Harold and also with deserting his Majesty's ship Australia and you are hereby fined 10/-."

The clerk stood up and said something to him but whatever it was he took no notice but commenced to tell me that just because I was a returned soldier didn't mean that I could go about the country robbing and intimidating people. He hoped that I would be properly dealt with when I returned to my ship, and I was to be attained until such time the naval authorities sent for me. The clerk got to his feet and spoke to him again at some length for he nodded and reluctantly asked me if I had anything to say. I said "look sir, those uniforms are my own and Harold did not object to me taking them, moreover, you have no right to try me until I have a naval officer here to represent me and also I was not asked to plead and no chance to make a defense, also, if you keep me here until the navy sends for me I will be an old man, you'll have to send me down under escort". He said, "is that all you have to say, constable take them away". Small took us out and locked us in a cell. Harold and Steve came, and Harold shamefacedly said, "I'll pay the fine", I said "not for me, you weren't a bloody fine cobber you've turned out to be, you know they're not your uniforms". He went red in the face and turned away, Steve said "are they his Harold?", but he wouldn't answer.

When teatime came Small came to the cell and gave us each a thick slice of bread very sparsely spread with butter and a tin cup of tea, each with no sugar or milk. I said to him "you are allowed 1/6 a meal to feed us and I want something better than this. He replied with "I know, but you'll go on wanting". "Well," I said, "if you think you are going to get the reward for capturing us, you've got another thing coming, we are only 72 hours adrift not deserters". He said no more but came back later and threw in two blankets each.

During the night Chris began to toss and turn and I asked him what was wrong. He said that he didn't feel well and was hot and feverish. I felt his forehead and he was as hot as first light. I yelled out for Small and when he came, I told him Chris had a fever, and when he looked at him he sure had and was covered in spots. He sent for Dr Boutman and he diagnosed German measles. He had Chris removed to hospital and placed the whole police station under two weeks quarantine. Small gave me breakfast of a thick slice of bread and dripping and a tin mug of tea, no milk or sugar, then he said, "you can work for your tucker if you want better than that, you start by cleaning the windows". I told him in straight forward language just what he could do with his windows and said that they'd better wake up to the fact that they had to send me to Sydney themselves.

To put a long story short, I put in a very idle fortnight, and the meals were always the same; bread and dripping for breakfast with tea, a meat sandwich and tea for dinner and bread with very little butter and tea for tea. Luckily the Muswellbrook Sergeant who apparently also controlled Singleton in those days came down with a constable and told me that the constable would take me to Sydney. I told him about the J.P and he said "don't worry, that won't stick. I also told him about the food, his only comment was "he still has the first sixpence he ever had". The constable and I went to Newcastle by train, and while there he took me into the waiting room and shouted me dinner, which in those days was a three-course meal at 2/-.

Arriving at Sydney and then tram to Circular Quay and ferry to the island. Here Mick took me before my engineer officer, who happened to be well under the influence when Mick pulled aside the curtain, he didn't recognize me, but curtly told Mick to put me in the cooler. Mick looked surprised but took me down to the lock up, he said "I've got to lock you up, so in you go, then I'll unlock it and if you turn up at the mess, I won't see you" a good bloke Mick, of course he locked me in after breakfast before rounds. When Kieghtley came the rounds with Mick, he spotted me in the cooler and said "what are you doing in there Honey?", I started to tell him that he'd put me there but Mick butted in and said "you weren't very well last night sir, so I thought it best sir", he replied "oh yes, well let the bloody man out, it's open arrest till the Aussie comes back".

Time passed fairly easily on the island. I wasn't supposed to go ashore in Sydney, and technically I wasn't supposed to do any work, but I soon found that I could be useful on the workboat which travelled around the harbour between Cockatoo and Goat islands with stores etc., otherwise life was quite easy. Just before the Aussie returned, Chris arrived back and was also placed under open arrest.

Immediately the old battle cruiser was tied up to No 1 buoy in Farm Cove. We were hustled aboard and taken before the Command by Shinez, Assistant Master at Arms. Shinez, who didn't like the stokers anyway, and me in particular, charged us as deserters.

The Commander just asked, "what have you to say?", "Not guilty Sir", "very well, Captain report". We marched back to the mess and later taken before the captain. This was Claude, an Englishman who was very much liked and known to be a very fair man, although strict. He addressed Shinez, "Master what is the charge?", "desertion Sir". Claude looked at Chris "what have you to say for yourself?", Chris was so scared he couldn't speak. The captain turned to me "perhaps you can speak", "yes sir, not guilty sir", Shinez chipped in "paper we used for the police report Sir", "No! I'll hear what this man has to say" then to me "Well! Let's hear your side first". I then told him that because we had been promised leave, because we had stood by the ship while in dock and had not received it we had decided to go A.W.L, that we were actually only 72 hours adrift and then I related exactly what occurred. Claude said, "you were actually locked up for a fortnight", "yes sir", "didn't you explain to the magistrate that you could not be tried civilly and must be returned to G. Island?", "yes sir but he wouldn't listen, he was only a J.P Sir", "very well, it seems you have been punished enough, but you know very well that you can't do as you please in the Navy, also you could always apply to me through the commander", "yes Sir, I did but Shinez here wouldn't accept our application, he said we'd have to wait until the ship returns from the cruise".

Claude looked at Shinez, "is this true Master", Shinez said "Well Sir, I believe there was some sort of application, but we were very busy at the time, and it was overloaded Sir", "very well, I'll go into that later" then to me "14 days 10a and you'd better collect your pay but what about the meals and reward?" I said, "I don't know about the reward Sir, but if there is one, it should go to the Constable who brought me from Singleton, as he was the one who caught us and also paid the 2/- for diner at Newcastle". Claude said "you know you have to pay for the meals at the police station", "yes Sir, if they had been meals, actually it was only bread, dripping and tea without sugar and milk", Claude said "you were only given bread and dripping, I was going to rule 1/6 per meal, but if that's true, we will refuse payment " "right, that's all. On caps, about turn, dismiss".

When we got out in the alley way Shinez said "you got away with it this time, but I'll get you yet". I made no reply but went below and raced forward to catch the paymaster before he closed his office. I had forgotten that while in dock the watertight doors had had six inches more plate welded all round, making them that much smaller and enabled them to be closed by one locking lever instead of 10 separate dog clips. The consequence was that leaping over the combing of the door, I clouted my head against the top and knocked myself out.

Luckily a seaman was behind me and picked me up. He was going to take me to sick bay, but I came to fairly quickly and said I would be alright. He steadied me until I got to the pay bob, who was just about to close, but I got my pay and bought a few things I was short of.

The seaman reported my fall and I had to report to the M.O, who made me stay in the sick bay until mess supper, but it did result in pads being placed on each side at the tops of the doors.

After this, Bill and I were put together again and we went back onto Auxiliary watchkeeping with a chap named Buttersby, a P.O stoker, a very nice chap and a good mate. Then the word went around that returned soldiers could cash their gratuities by using it as a deposit on land or a house. So, I went to Peach Bros estate agents in Sydney and bought a block of land out at Hurstville on what was known then as the Peakhurst Park Estate. I paid £50 for it and got a receipt but the deeds had to be made out and signed and these were not ready. I was told that it would probably take a month or six weeks. I was not very worried, money or the lack of it never troubled me, if you had, well and good and if you hadn't, it didn't matter. Had I had any sense or had thought to look into the future, I had a wonderful opportunity then to make a start for a settled life, but I was young, getting on for 21 and couldn't have cared less about the future. Moreover, I was restless and wanted to see the country and other lands.

Well Bill, P.O Battersby and I decided we would go and have a look at the block of land. So, we hired a horse and sulky from the stables near the brewery. It was a beautiful afternoon and we bought six bottles of beer, two of orangeade, a lobster, and a whole stack of sandwiches and we set off to Hurstville. The trouble began when the pony drew into a pub and before he would shift, we had to get a switch and that's how it went as we approached the pub. The pony would make straight for, and we'd have to use the switch before he'd go on. Eventually we arrived, of course then it was all bush and we had to hunt around a bit before we located the pegs. This done, we decided to have our picnic, giving the pony his nose bag after giving him a drink from a little spring on the block, then we settled down to eat.

Bill got stuck into the beer and after one glass Battersby shared the orangeade with me. Batt was a pommy and probably thought the beer 2nd grade. I never touched the stuff, Bill ended up drinking all the beer while Batt and I cleared up the lobster and the sandwiches. Bill of course was dead drunk and went to sleep and as it had taken longer than expected to get out there, we decided that we'd better start home.

Halfway home Bill woke up and started singing at the top of his voice and shouting out to everyone we passed. Batt threatened to knock him out, but he took no notice until at last he went to sleep again, nearly falling out of the sulky. Thankfully, we arrived back at the stables, collected our deposit of £1 and getting a taxi we went back to the ship. Before getting into the picket boat at Man-o-war steps Bat gave Bill a thump on the back and Bill was very sick, which luckily enabled him to straighten up enough to pass the gangway without being logged by the Quartermaster. I never signed the deeds for the land as by the time they were ready, I was no longer in Sydney.

Bill had a younger brother, Ned, working in Sydney as a blacksmith's striker and we met him at the Mission to Seaman. Bill told me that Ned had got a girl into trouble in Springhurst where they lived. The girl that was a neighbour, claimed that Ned was the father. Ned denied this, saying that she had been with so many boys that any one of them could be the father, and as the girl, who through her mother had taken a court order against him, he'd left in a hurry, gone to Sydney and got this job as a striker. He and I became friendly, and he used to come aboard sometimes. I was off watch, but life became very boring and monotonous for me. Swinging around the buoy at Farm Cove, going ashore every 2nd day, staying overnight at Naval House and going aboard at 7am the next morning to start the 8am shift. I never bothered with girls as the others did, and I didn't know any anyway. I saw the zoo, went for trips to the Hawksberry and Narrabeen and out to Daceyville but there's no fun in seeing things on your own and I very soon got sick of it.

Then one evening Paddy, one of our mess mates asked me to go ashore with him. Bill always went off by himself, he was a real ladies' man and I usually stayed aboard and played cards or mooched around the gardens or went to the theatre.

Paddy and I were walking up George Street towards the state theatre after booking in at Naval House, when two young girls, who couldn't have been more than 14 or 15 stopped Paddy and asked him if he could help them. I asked them what the trouble was, and they had told us that their landlady had locked them out and they had nowhere to go. Paddy was all for taking them to a hotel, but I pointed out that two young sailors couldn't barge into a hotel with two young girls. Boy was I naïve. I had the solution, as a child, we'd always been taught that if we were in trouble to ask a policeman and my own experience had shown me that police were always kind and helpful. So, the obvious solution, the police station, and that's where we took them. The Sergeant looked a bit surprised when we walked in and I explained the trouble, pointing out that I'd always been taught to go to the police, and I thought that it was the best thing to do.

Paddy said, "You're bloody mad, we could have had a night with those girls". Then I realized why he was reluctant to go to the station, so I said, "they are only kids, and if they are dinkum they've got nothing to fear and will be looked after and if they are not then we are well rid of them, they could cause serious trouble for us". Paddy never asked me to go ashore with him again and I wouldn't have gone if he'd asked.

The consequence was that most of the mess thought I was crackers and wouldn't go ashore with me, so life was fairly quiet. Bat asked me one night if I have ever had a woman and when I said no, he asked me why. I said that I didn't know any, that the only one I had known had dumped me because I was a common sailor. Apart from which, if he had been in the Army Medical Corps, as I had and seen the results of promiscuity in Bulford venereal hospital, he'd be wary of them too.

Looking back, I can see now why I got so fed up with the Navy that I left. I didn't drink or smoke, didn't go near woman, and although the boys were friendly enough, when I asked anyone to go ashore with me, they always had some reason for not going. So, I was more or less quite lonely at times and doing nothing but swinging around the buoy in Farm Cove wasn't my idea of Navy life.

Anyway, going ashore one Saturday I met Ned Jenvey and mentioned to him that I was just about fed up with the navy and thought I'd give it away. He said, "if you go, I'll come with you and we'll go to Springhurst to my place, my trouble should have blown over by now". I agreed and we arranged that when I came off watch on Sunday evening, I'd book in at Naval House for the night and we'd leave on Monday morning. After purchasing a civvy coat, hat and trousers, this we did. We caught a train to Corowa and walked from there from Springhurst, staying overnight at Rutherglen.

I was made very welcome by Ned's parents, especially his father, who was an Englishmen from Southampton, he had been out here many years. He had married, and he and his wife had reared a family of ten. Stan the eldest was married, Eva the next was married to a wheat expert at Rutherglen College, Tom. More of those two later. Next was Bill, then Fred, then Ned, then Margie 16, then Jimmy,14, then Dores. I forgot Ivy, who came between Bill and Fred and was married to Rocky and living at Springhurst.

After the introductions I got to know the family well. The old man was a farmer who had bought his farm from a landowner named Tyrell and was just about at the point of total ownership, when he would pay his last installment in the coming harvest, which he eventually did.

Now we found that far from Ned's trouble having passed away, they were well and truly still there. The girl's mother who lived on an adjoining farm heard that Ned was home and the next thing, he received a summon to appear in court at Wangaratta, which he did, as I pointed out that it was better to face the music and take the medicine or else marry the girl. He refused to marry her on the grounds that too many boys had been intimate with her. Everyone thought that all that would happen would be that he'd have to pay for maintenance. Ned was 19 and he swore that the girl was 18 but the mother came to court with a certificate purporting to show that at the time of intimacy the girl had only been 16, the result being that the judge sentenced him to 6 months in prison.

While Ned was serving his sentence, I stayed on with the Jenvey's helping the old man. Fred and I learned to sit on a horse, drive a team and plow. I didn't ask for wages and didn't get any, I was treated as part of the family. We were a few miles from Springhurst, between there and Chiltern, we could see the mullock heaps from the Console Mines in the distance, only a mile or so away. I liked the farm work, especially at harvest time. The old man was an expert rick builder and was in demand by the surrounding farmers at harvest time to build their hay and wheat stacks. The old man took pains to teach me the proper way to build a stack. I revelled in the work and went with him to help the harvest on the adjoining farms. One of the farms was owned by a widow and all the farmers around joined in to take her harvest in. all she had to do was feed us and although this meant practically 5 meals a day, she had the other woman to help. Then we worked on Bill Baker's farm, and I was paid the greatest compliment I've ever received when on paying us off, he offered me his checkbook and told me to write my own check, of course I couldn't, so he paid me 15/- a day instead of 12/6 which was the ruling rate then.

After 4 months Ned was released on parole and came home. His brother Fred had made his fiancé pregnant, married her and on a farm a mile down the road for a family named Withers on Wages.

In the meantime, I had started a market garden on a water reserve up on the edge of the forest and Bill was backing me to apply for 10 acres of it, for that purpose he took the round to meet the Shire councilors and get their approval. When that was settled, I went to the Lands Board, they knocked me back so I tackled the Repatriation committee, they also knocked me back, but said would I consider wheat farming; there were other applicants for various reasons, but all were knocked back, but asked to consider wheat farming. We put our heads together and decided that if the committee would locate us all in one area, where we could work together and help each other, we would take it on but this they flatly refused and said we would have to go where sent and we would not all be in the one area. These committee members were city businessmen and simply hadn't a clue about farming. One man with us had a farm in Gippsland, his father had started him off with a few cows and he wanted the £640 allowed to buy a pure-bred bull to upgrade his heard. These men told him that it was ridiculous to pay that much for a bull and they wouldn't hear of it. So, we all came away empty-handed and we went back to Springhurst.

Bill then came to me and told me he'd bought the Wilters paddocks, and if I liked to take it on the shares, he'd take me into Wangaratta and guarantee me £500 with the bank to get me started and obtain the necessary gear. Old man Jenvey offered me the loan of ploughs etc. until I could get some of my own.

This put me in a spot as Fred had been working the property and naturally thought that he would be allowed to keep on it, also he was my friend and his father had been very good to me. I knew that he was disappointed that Fred hadn't been given the chance although he'd generously offered me the use of horses and machinery.

I walked up and down the yard that night sorely tempted to take the offer, but I knew I couldn't do it, although had I known the outcome, I would have taken it. As it was, I went to Bill and told him that Fred expected to be given the chance that he was married and had a wife and child to care for and I couldn't take it from him. Bill pointed out that the property was his and he was not bound to any particular person, and he could place who he liked on it and he was sure I could make a go of it, but as I wouldn't take it up, he'd give Fred the chance.

The very next day Bill took Fred into Wangaratta and guaranteed him to the bank and Fred came and thanked me very profusely for turning the offer down, then to my disgust, went into town and bought a brand-new flash rubber tyred sulky. I admit that he had the use of his father's plant, but any good farmer would have continued to use the old sulky and bought his own horses and machinery, after all, the old sulky was good enough to go courting in.

When Ned arrived home, things had changed, his sister Eva and Tom, who was over 60, Eva being 22, had left Rutherglen College because of a young man with a degree in Agriculture had been appointed manager over Tom's head and Tom wouldn't work under him. Tom had at first bought rabbit traps, a shotgun and a hooded wagon and trekked down to Bairnsdale Way, doing no good there, he took on a job as carpenters' labourer but was too particular and slow. He had to leave that but had then gone on to Redcliffs near Mildura and started as a building contractor. He was a very clever old man and could turn his hand to anything. He had been a wheat breeding expert at a college in South Africa, but in Redcliffs he was in a Returned Soldiers Settlement and needed a returned man to cover the contract and having heard about me, though I hadn't met him, Eva wrote and suggested we go and get work there. Ned was only too willing, and I had no objections.

CHAPTER FOURTEEN: CLOSING OLD CHAPTERS

I must go back a bit as while Ned was in goal, I was picked up by two detectives from Rutherglen and taken to Williamstown Naval Depot. There I was paraded before Commander Hare and without asking for any defense or reason, sentenced to 28 days detention and discharge from the Navy. This suited me as it left me completely free from them and at the same time excluded me from any reserve call up.

I didn't serve the full 28 days, the Governor of the goal treated it more as a rest cure, not allowing me to mix with other civilian prisoners and employed me to do various odd jobs around the place. One job was to replace the light bulbs on the top of the high wall, there were quite a number of these at intervals around the 20ft wall and I had to use a long ladder. The Governor was a nice old chap and was very conscious of his responsibilities and as he said, I wasn't a criminal and he wasn't going to treat me like one. I ate my meals in the wardens' messroom and was never locked up. Commander Hare would have had a fit if he'd known how I was treated. One of the wardens showed me the death cell and the rope that hung Ned Kelly, but I wasn't very impressed as at that time I knew very little about Kelly.

It was while I was there that the Governor brought me the telegram informing me of mum's death and I felt very depressed for quite a while, as I never appreciated all she had done for me and my thoughtlessness and selfishness in not going home before we left for Australia was nagging at my conscience. It had not, until that moment, occurred to me that she loved me, all that I ever saw when I thought about her was a picture of her standing over me with a fork in her hand, threatening to gouge my eyes out and to this day, I don't know what for. Bert says it was something to do with him and Jim raiding the condensed milk tin and I got the blame, all I know was that I'd just got in the door, walked halfway down the passage when mum knocked me flat on my back and then stood over me, threatening me with the fork. Now looking back, I can understand the terrible struggle. She was constantly waging to keep us fed and clothed on dad's pitiful wage of 35/- a week, and sometimes if he'd managed to get a new customer, a little bit of commission. But because of that, mum had to pay 12/5 a week rent to the Duchy of Cornwall's agent, as all the property was owned by the Prince of Wales.

On top of that, she had to pay for gas, firewood, coal and feed four boys and dad. How she managed it, I'll never know. When Alf left school and got a job that helped a bit and Will of course also helped. He was an artificial arm and leg maker and worked in the Strand.

But to get back to tors. At the end of 24 days the Governor called me to his office and gave me my Naval discharge and 72/- £3-12's, my wages of 3/- a day while in the goal, wished me the best of luck and escorted me out to the gate, shook hands and said goodbye.

I went straight to the station and back to Springhurst. I had been given a voucher to take me to Sydney, as that was where I had joined but I left the train at Springhurst and walked up to Rocky Tomkin's place, which was only about ½ a mile from the station. They welcomed me back and gave me lunch and then Ivy drove me to the old man's place, where I received a tumultuous welcome from the family and fell back into place, just as if I'd never been away.

So, Ned and I went back to Melbourne, and then on to Redcliffs, which at that time was all Mallee scrub on red sandy soil. The soil was alright, lack of water was the trouble, and the commission was cutting irrigation channels from the Murray, but first the mallee scrub had to be cleared. When we arrived, the first 33,000 acres on the eastern side of the line was in the process of finalizing the clearing. All timber suitable for fence posts, stay post or poles were cut and carved away. The stumps were in the process of being stacked and burned, this was done by many gangs of returned men, eight or so in each gang, who stacked the stumps and fired them, this was a great lurk. The men stood around the fires poking at them with poles when they got tired of standing at one fire, they'd move onto another to give it a few pokes and for this they were paid 12/6 a day.

Being a returned soldier, I was able to sign a sub-contract to clear land for the big machine known as "Big Lizzie". This consisted of three huge tanks built of steel. They stood about 10ft to the deck, on one was a big Blackstone engine under a shed. This had a huge fly wheel about 8ft in diameter and drove the machine by gears and cogs through the huge rear wheels. Each wheel was really like two wheels as they were very wide and were fitted with shallow punt like shoes. Three to each wheel about 4ft long and held to the wheel by very heavy steel cable. The rear wheels each had two sets of these shoes and when the machine travelled, each wheel left a track you could nearly drive a sulky down. The machine with the engine towed the other two when travelling; they all had similar wheels. A second tank had a house built on it and the third had two 4,000-gallon tanks, side by side.

The whole lot was built by a German engineer, Bottrell, he was a seventh day Adventists and built the machines to originally cart metal across the Murray. The engine proved ideal for the purpose of clearing, for while it only travelled at 4 miles an hour, it was powerful enough to pull enough stumps to clear over an acre every move. This was achieved by means of heavy wire ropes. There were two of these attached to the front of "Big Lizzie" and four or five for the rear. Two men dragged the two front ropes and wound them in and out among as many stumps as possible, hooking them onto a big stump. Bottnell then moved backwards while the men on the rear ropes wound them in and out as many stumps as possible, hooking them onto a big stump where possible. This resulted in the stumps in the front flying out of the ground as the ropes in front straightened until the anchor stumps also pulled out. Then Bottrell would drive forward, and the process would be repeated in the rear. Our job, Ned, and I, was to go ahead and cut everything at breast height and recover any timber that would cut into a pole, a post or if big enough, a strainer post. We started days before Big Lizzie had finished on the Eastern side of the line.

I had never used an axe before and although my hands weren't soft, I soon gathered a crop of blisters. To make it worse the axe was a 3lb Kelly, not really heave enough for the work. At first I couldn't hit in the same place twice but I soon learned the knack of it, although for the first three days it took all my will power to keep going, my hands getting raw and bleeding, but they hardened up and I started to really enjoy the work; the timber was mostly mallee gum with a fair amount of sandalwood and cypress pine. The pine was easy, the sandalwood fairly hard, the red and white mallee quite hard and the black mallee a real bitch, but it made very good mauls, and it was the black mallee that tested me. We were paid the fixed rate of 12/6 a day by Bottrell, who had a fixed contract to clear

33,000 on the West side of the line after he had finished the East side 33,000 acres.

One morning, only a day or two after we had started, Ned and I went out as usual and I found myself in a clump of black mallee gum. This was the first time I had struck these trees. The mallee gums grow in clumps, usually four to six trees in a clump, each one varying from six to eight inches through, so one has a certain amount of difficulty in getting a clear go at them. This particular morning, I walked around the clump seeking the best position in which to swing the axe, then getting a good grip on the handle, I swung at the nearest trunk. There was a ringing sound, and a great chunk flew out of the axe face. I'd cut too straight instead of on aslant, and of course, learnt a lesson and ruined an axe. I called Ned and he came over and said, "I'll bet those are black mallee's", I said "They're grey, not black and hard as hell". He cut into the tree, he was a superb axe man and showed me the wood. It was a very dark grey and sure hard enough for anyone.

Ned said we'd have to have new heavy axes. So, we knocked off and went to a store set up in a shed near the railway station by two brothers and they let us have two 4 ½ lb Plumb axes on credit. This put a different complexion on things and as soon as I got the feel of the new axe, we soon started to literally make a hole in the scrub. It was hard but healthy work. My hands developed corns and my shoulders strengthened and toughtened. Well, the day came when we finished our falling work for Bottnell and he paid us off. So, we decided to have a day in town and buy ourselves some more gear. To this end, I went to the Commission Office and signed a contract to clear a 400-acre strip that is an area 40 chains long by 10 wide. That being done we went to Mildura to shop, taking old Tom and his wife Eva with us.

Ned and I bought two 4lb axes for felling, keeping the 4 ½lb for logging. Plum axes of course, a set of six wedges and maul rings, we made our own mauls from black mallee, 1 man M tooth saws about 4ft long and we also bought a horse worked Trewella tree grubber. We also bought a few household items for Eva as a gift for looking after us. Tom bought a sturdy young draft horse and light wagon or cart. These things besides hammers, saws, nails etc. were put in the cart. Tom drove home while Eva, Ned and I waited to go back on the train, in the meantime, having a look around the town and having lunch.

The next day Ned and I went out with the surveyors to mark out our 40-chain strip and then we set to work falling the timber. We decided to clear a 10c x 10c area first before we brought in the horse grubber and in the meantime to Tom wired his two sons by his marriage to come up to Redcliff, by the time they arrived, Ned and I had cut all the trees in the first 10 x 10 chain area. So, we then brought in the grubber and with the two boys on the wire ropes, Ned driving the horse and I working the grubber, we proceeded to clear the stumps. Here a description of the grubber may not go amiss, it consisted of two cotton shaped metal plates between which the cogs were mounted, so! The ½ inch wire went around the large pulley wheel on top held in place by a guide, this wire had eye pieces at each end into which the single bar hook was placed. After the men had taken the stump wire in and around as many stumps as possible, the hand was used to tighten this wire and if the stumps did not pull out, the horse was hooked onto the horse wire and driven away. The gears gave the horse tremendous power and the stumps usually fell out of the ground. Usually, we could pull most mallee stumps with the handle. It was the Sandalwood and pine stumps that needed the horse.

We had cleared about 4 ½ acres, when the surveyors came over and told us to leave a strip four chains wide, right down the middle of the 40-acre strip. I pointed out that we already cut down the trees in the first 10 x 10. They said, "That's alright but leave all the trees in a 40 strip down the middle from there on". I said, "We have a contract for 40 x 10 chain £12 an acre". They assured me that we would be paid for the lot, so we carried on. We worked on with the stump pulling with the first 10 chains and congratulated ourselves for getting paid for not felling trees in the four-chain strip, when a few days later the chief surveyor came over and told us to knock off. The government had run out of money and all work had to cease. I asked, "what about the contract?", he said, "That's ok, you'll be paid" and believe it or not, we were paid £480 for 10 acres cut down and about 5 ½ acres cleared. The thing I didn't understand is why since they had to pay us. They didn't insist on us finishing the job, we offered to, but they gave us the check and cancelled the contract.

Now we had agreed that Ned and I would do all the falling and Tom's two boys would only be paid for the work on the stumps. We agreed that the falling work was the hardest and should take 2/3rd of the money. So, Ned and I took £150 each for the felling, and £180 was divided between the four of us, so the two boys got £45 each for their work. Ned and I agreed that our £45 each was enough, and we wouldn't take into account the use of the grubber and Tom wouldn't charge us for the horse and cart.

I had no bank account, so I endorsed the check and Tom paid it into his bank account and then the trouble arose. He wanted us to leave the money with him, and he said he would invest it for us. The others agreed to let him do that but I refused. Tom was over 62 and could die and I might never see my share and anyway, I had no intention of staying at Redcliff. The commission had asked me to take up one of the blocks, but I refused, besides, I had worked a week or so with Tom and he was old, slow and pernickety. I didn't trust him or his wife, so I insisted on getting my money and very grudgingly he gave me his check for £205, which I promptly cashed.

In the six months or so at Redcliff I did fairly well. I went into Mildura with Ned and we each had a suit made and bought new shoes and socks. By the time I collected these I finished up with a metal cabin trunk full of tools; 2 axes, maul and wedges, carpenters' tools, a 4-foot 6 inch one man saw, a new outfit and about £100 in the Commonwealth savings bank.

I elected to go back to Springhurst as the old man had written and asked us to go back for the harvest. Ned wouldn't go but he decided to go back to Gippsland with Tom's two sons. So, we parted company, and I went back to Springhurst and went to work on the harvest. Fred had apparently also settled down and also worked on the harvest, but he wasn't a constant worker. He was too fond of driving into town to see the pictures or go dancing with his wife, his sisters doing the babysitting. Eventually the harvesting ended, like a goat having what I considered lots of money, I lent money to Fred and also let him use my carpenter's tools as he was doing a bit of building on his place.

I had after the harvest pulled down a two roomed place. The old man had bought from down the road a mile and re-erected it at the back of the old home, where after we had built a big open fireplace and chimney at one end and installed a stove. It became a very roomy kitchen and another bedroom, while the old kitchen became a bedroom.

Then Ned came home again and suggested that his eldest brother Stan, himself, and I should take on woodcutting for Cock's Pioneer Gold and Tin mining company of Eldorado, and this we did. We camped six miles from Springhurst in the forest and each of us were allotted a strip 10 chains wide and 50 chains long. Then the ranger went through and marked all the straightest trees, which were not to be cut and numbered them with a stamp

I had for a while, before Ned returned, cut box trees for firewood in a paddock just below Springhurst at 7/- a cord, and had made myself a 10ft x 12ft tent from duck canvas with 6ft walls. This, together with my woodcutting tools and a stretcher I carted through to my new campsite and started work. This time I worked alone but Ned and Stan worked together. The reason being that I was not in the same class as an axe man and as we were paid 6/6 a cord and had no advantage here as I was the holder of the contract one could not blame them for working by themselves. I believe that given a little time I could have matched either of them but here the conditions were different and harder.

We had to cut within six inches of the ground and do what they called mellanising, this consisted of leaving the stump with an equal slope of cut on each side. This enabled the rain to roll off and the stump then shot new shots, sometimes two or three shoots to each stump. This resulted in a very thick strand of trees thus causing them to grow straight.

The only trouble with this method of cutting from the cutter's point of view was that he had to bend to cut, and unless he could use both hands to do alternate sides, then he had to trim the stump to the satisfaction of the forester. Luckily, I was born left-handed, although compelled to use my right at school, so that, I found no difficulty in changing the position of my hands on the axe without shifting my position. So, I cut left and right but it took time to learn this new method of felling, also big trees had to be split into sizeable billets so they could be easily handled by the men stoking the boilers. Moreover, the billets had to be stoked between two sticks so they could be measured in ¼ ½ and 1 cord heaps. All billets had to be cut to standard length, which was if I remember rightly either 3ft or 3ft 6in. a chord would then be 7ft 2in long, and 18in height. To make wages as they were then, one had to cut 2 ½ cords a day. That meant felling the trees, measuring and cutting to length, trimming and stacking the bushes in tidy heaps, splitting any big billets and stacking the billets between the two sticks in the ground at the proper distance. 6l a cord was retained until winter when one was expected to go out and burn, under supervision, all the bushes.

It was hard work. No one knows what hard work really means until he has cut 2 ½ cords of wood under those conditions in the height of summer. I was just at the point where I could hope to cut my 2 ½ cords each day when I received a letter from brother Bert, who had come out under the Dreadnough boys scheme and had been training at

Scheyville Agriculture College in N.S.W but had been farmed out to a farmer at Tarago N.S.W who was apparently a bit of a slave driver, imploring me to rescue him. I suspect that he was a bit homesick too, and anyway I sent him £5 and told him to come along.

Somehow my money earned at Redcliffe and various jobs had more or less evaporated. I've never set much store by it anyway, but when Bert arrived, I had to buy a few things for him besides extra food. So, I had to go on credit with the storekeeper and I found that as an axe man Bert would have made a good storekeeper. He didn't seem to get the left and right manner of cutting, so I gave him the job of splitting the big logs. I never slit a log if I could lift it, but forgetting that, I'd probably been the same when I started. Bert would split logs that I would have tossed on the heap, so I put him to work stacking bushes and the billets. That ws alright but to just feed ourselves meant that I had to cut at least three cords a day for 7 days a week. Then we had to lose a day a week to walk the six miles into Springhurst for supplies and to this end I got a pair of old sulky wheels and axle and made a shaft from a pole, some packing case wood made a floor, and we towed that in and out to Springwood on Saturday. Then the storekeeper told me I owed £12 and altogether with the butcher and the baker my debts came to nearly £20, and I wasn't able to average three cords a day.

So, I decided to cut my losses and leave for N.S.W. I worked out that my tent was worth at least £12, and the storekeeper would certainly sell it for more. Axes, wedges, crowbar and my tools left with Fred I reckoned would more than cover what I owed. So, we walked over to Eldorada Office and collected my money. I told them that I was leaving so they only paid me 6/- a cord and I ended up with about £12 ad Bert had the hide to ask me for half, well, he had nothing, so we halved the money and walking through the bush to Chiltern, we caught a train to Albury then to Sydney.

There we contacted the employment bureau which was then situated in George Street North, and we were advised to go out to Bankstown to where the Catholic Convent is now. It was then all the bush and then in the process of being cleared; we saw the contractor and asked for a three-year contract. He refused but offered us 7/- a ton for all wood cuts. We refused this as we had no axes or maul and wedges, and would have had to buy new ones, as Bert wasn't an axe man, and we would have been working in competition with other cutters. We would have been lucky to make wages and the job would have been cut out before Bert became expert enough and we would have bought our gear for no purpose.

So, we left Bankstown and reported back to Mr. Belmore at the employment exchange. There were no jobs going that we could take for two so we decided that we would have to separate. Bert was offered and took a farming job at Leeton, and I took on a job as ploughman at a station out from Junee. Mr. Belmore told me that the job was supposed to be permanent and gave both of us rail warrants, Bert's for Leeton and mine for Junee.

We travelled in the same train that night and parted company at Junee where I got off. I was met at the station by a young man in a sulky, Wilfred. He said that he was welcoming me on behalf of his eldest brother, Walter, who had been a tally clerk at Yarmouth in England until brought out by his father who had come out some years before and taken up land on part of a large station. The owner of which had been given the choice of sub-dividing the station into 640-acre blocks for wheat farming or being taken over by the Government. Naturally he chose to subdivide, and Wilfred's father had leased one to his second son, Brock, Jack another and the third had been leased on behalf of Walter who had a pisa house built for him by his father and bringing his wife and children with him, had started on the work of clearing and plowing. He had asked the Labour Exchange to send him an Englishman for a permanent plowman. He himself was no real worker, and in fact only wanted a man to burn up the stumps on the first 50 acres and had his young son plowing 25 of them; had he asked for a temporary hand, he would not have got it, as in those days the exchange would only supply hands on a permanent basis.

All this I discovered later. I got on well with Wilfred and on the way out to Murrulebale station, which I believe was the name of the homestead, we quickly took a liking to each other, and we joked and sang our way to his home. On arrival I was met by his father and mother who gave me a hearty welcome and a meal. That afternoon they tried to round up a cow to milk, the cow had different ideas, and as there was no bale, we had quite a circus as she chased each one of us in turn as we tried to get her against a big box tree where Wifred usually milked her. In the end she chased me, then I got mad and picked up a pitchfork, and holding with a rifle and bayonet at the charge with the tines turned down, I stood and faced her. Wilfred's father yelled not to hurt her, but I couldn't have cared less as I was really mad at being chased by a cow. The result was that she lowered her head and charged straight into the tines. She must have got a shock for she had turned calmly around, walked over to the tree, and stood to be milked. Wilfred later told me that she never again attempted to charge anyone, so long as someone had a pitchfork handy.

Later that day I was taken over to Walyers selection, introduced to Wilfred's father and shown my bedroom. He asked me what part of England I had come from and when I told him London, he seemed quite satisfied. I didn't tell him that I'd been here since 1916 and had been in the A.I.F and the Navy and he quite naturally thought that I was a raw new chum, and I made no effort to disillusion him. He was to pay me £2 a week and keep and if I stayed for six months, he was to refund the fare to the exchange. When I asked him about the plowing, he was very evasive and said that would depend on how I got on. His wife was a thin sallow woman, who was continually complaining about the heat, the dust, the wind, and the flies, certainly they were a nuisance, but one gets used to them and complaining doesn't help, so I kept very much to myself. I offered no comment and said as little as possible, while she continually harped on wanting to go back to England, it was not a happy house.

Next day Wilfred's father said he was going into Junee and I asked him to get me a pair of ex army boots at the disposal store to which he agreed and I would pay him the 12/6 when I got my pay, but first he took me down the paddock and showed me how the stumps were to be burned out and telling his 12 year old boy to go on with the plowing he went off to Junee.

I worked like a beaver that day digging round stumps and carrying logs and hot coals from one to another and I really did work hard for I liked the other Brocks, the father and mother, and Jack and Wilfred but I quickly saw that Wilfred's father was no toiler. He left all the digging and carrying of logs and wood to me and just carted coals from one fire to another or stood and poked them up,

This went on for a fortnight and then this particular morning while we were eating breakfast he had a

196

real white-hot row with his wife, she moaning that she wanted to go back to England and nagging him about it, so that he got up, left his breakfast and stalked off down the paddock. I finished my breakfast, picked up my shovel and axe and followed him.

I knew that the burning off was finished, and I intended to ask him about the plowing, since the only plow was being used by the lad and there was no other and no more horses. He had stopped about halfway down the rise and said, "you're no good to me, you're too lazy", I said "is that so, well how come you've never caught up with me? I think you're a bloody twister and never had any intention of having a permanent plowman", "That's right" he said, "and I'm only going to pay you 30/- less the 12/6 for the boots", I said "you contracted to pay me £2 a week and keep, and you can't take anything from my wages, so you've got your choice. I'm no Tommy new chum to be taken in by you, I'm an ex-A.I.F man and ex-navy and you pay the £4 for the fortnight or take the consequences". He made a swing at me with the shovel, it caught my arm and I saw red. I tore into him with all I had and was vaguely aware of his wife yelling at me to kill the bugger. I don't think he got one blow in from that moment but when he'd had enough, I'd knocked him to the ground, and he got up. I marched him up to the house and stood over him while he wrote the cheque for £4. I told him that he'd better go back to England for if a genuine Aussie got to him, he'd get both his head and ribs kicked in, all he had were bruiser and a black eye. He asked me if I was going to pay for the boots, I said I'll send you the money when I cash the cheque and I really meant to but killed the idea when he said, "You can find your own bloody way to Junee".

I could have gone to Wilfred or the old man, but I realized that it would only make family trouble, so I set off to walk to the road which was a good way off past the homestead.

I had to go through Jack's selection, and he was busy fencing. I stopped and asked him the way and naturally he wanted to know what had happened. I told him the whole thing and he said, "Why not come and work for me, Walter will never do any good, he's too lazy and besides has only ever done office work before". I pointed out that it would only cause family trouble and besides, I really preferred to work on the coast.

Jack wished me all the best and I went on my way. It was hot, dry, and dusty and I had quite a sweat up and as I passed the Homestead I decided to go in and get a drink of water, which I did. The owner came out and gave me a glass of water and asked me "wasn't I the man working with Walter?", I said I was, and he asked me where I was going, of course that led to me having to tell the reason again. He said, "I thought you a good enough worker, why not stay and take up one of the remaining blocks?". I pointed out that I had no money, and, in any case, it would be awkward for Brock's. He remarked that he didn't think Wilfred's father would make a go of it and he might have to let him go. I stuck to my refusal to stay, and he then directed me to the road and said that the mail sulky would be along presently and to tell the mailman to take me into Junee. So, I trudged on and soon after striking the road, along came the mail sulky and that took me to Junee. I had lunch at the hotel and then caught the train to Sydney.

CHAPTER FIVETEEN: NEW BEGINNINGS

When I saw Mr. Belmore at the exchange the next day and told him the story, he wiped Wilfred's fathers name off the list and said he'd never be listed again and moreover would get a bill for my fare to Junee. He then said he had an application for a farm hand who was a protestant and could milk and preferably English, for a place on the North Coast at a place called Lansdown on the manning River. I was a bit suspicious but decided to take it and caught the North Coast Rail that night.

I arrived at Lansdown late the next evening. The month was September 1922 and was met at the station by big Jim Pereira, my new boss. After picking up a few things at the store we drove out to the farm. Jim told me he was working a farm on ½ shares for two Batchelor brothers named Newby.

On arrival at the farm as I got down from the sulky, I became aware that a girl and a woman had come out on the verandah. When I was introduced to them, I realized that the girl was a real beauty and I think I fell for her right at that moment. I was practically adopted into the family and then we discovered that we were both in love with each other. We were given every encouragement by her mother.

I worked with the family up till the beginning of June, and of course the inevitable happened, we became lovers, then the blow fell. Jim was given notice to quit the farm and it turned out that he only had an unwritten agreement with Newby's, nothing in writing. I had to leave and went to Sydney to obtain a job on a poultry farm in the day-old chick trade. Naomi also came to Sydney and started a position with a family as a maid. She came to see me at the poultry farm and told me she was pregnant. There was only one solution, we had to marry and this, with the help of the family she worked for, we did, at St Mathias church Paddington on June 28th, 1923. Naomi continued to work with the family who were very good to her. I continued to work on the poultry farm and learned the day-old chick trade and poultry farming generally.

I then made an application for a block of land at Galston and this was approved. It was I think 1 ½ acres and was immediately adjoining the night soil depot, which was to be added later. Bert had joined us by then and worked on the poultry farm. We agreed that Bert would continue on the farm and Naomi with the family, and I would leave and plant passion fruit on the Galston block, but all this depended on me getting the returned soldier's loan of £625. So, I went into the repeat and was asked what I proposed to do with the money. I explained my ideas and there was a lot of humming and ha Ing, then I was asked "had I considered wheat farming?". I said "yes!" but considered that under the circumstances I'd do better with poultry and passionfruit, more humming and ha-ing so I lost patience and demanded straight out "Did I get the money or not?", eventually they said "No". so, I walked out and I went back to Dick McNuce and told him, he said "There's a Mr. Nelson has been out here with the papers for you to sign for the £625". I stormed back to Sydney and went in and when I saw the loan officer, I asked him "Did his right hand know what his left hand did?". So, I told him in no uncertain terms what I thought of him and the whole shebang, he took it very well but said that I was more suited to wheat farming. The upshot was that I went around to the Murrumbidgee offices and got the forms to apply for a block. I sent a note to Judge Edwards relinquishing the Galston block and told him why.

The forms for the Bidgee blocks were very closely printed, 3 foolscap size, most in small print, so I set to closely study them and I discovered that they were for a 99 year lease and could be recalled on six months' notice, that the board at any time could take possession of any portion if so required for irrigation or other purposes, could take over any building of any kind for whatever purpose. In other words, they were giving themselves an open-handed cheque, and I told them so. I wasn't very tactful and as now been seen, all the poor devils who took up blocks of 640 acres and didn't read the fine print were shunted off and eventually it was sold to the Italians.

After many endeavours and multiple jobs later, I secured a position as a labourer with the rail laying gang and was appointed fettler at Wollongong.

The journey of soul-led endeavours led to the most alluring circumstances. Life is simple with the consciousness of presence.

Quite the journey I had looking back but the most joy that I ever did experience was that of love and simplicity.